STEPHEN CRANE

Literature and Life: American Writers

Selected list of titles in this series:

Complete list of titles in the series available from the publisher on request.

STEPHEN CRANE

Bettina L. Knapp

UNGAR • NEW YORK

My deepest thanks go to Alba Amoia for her wise counsel in the preparation of this volume.

1987
The Ungar Publishing Company
370 Lexington Avenue, New York, NY 10017

Printed in the United States of America

Library of Congress Cataloging-in-Publication Data

Knapp, Bettina Liebowitz, 1926–
    Stephen Crane.

    (Literature and life. American writers)
    Bibliography: p.
    Includes index.
    1. Crane, Stephen, 1871–1900 — Criticism and interpretation. I. Title. II. Series.
PS1449.C85Z715   1987   813'.4   86-25113
ISBN 0-8044-2468-3

Contents

Chronology

1871   Stephen Crane is born on November 1, in Newark, New Jersey, to Rev. Dr. Jonathan Townley Crane and Mary Helen Peck Crane.

1878   Dr. Crane becomes Methodist minister in Port Jervis, New York, the "Whilomville" of Crane's tales. Crane begins school.

1880   Death of Dr. Crane on February 16.

1882   Mrs. Crane moves to Asbury Park, New Jersey. Crane goes to school there until 1888.

1885   Crane writes his first story, "Uncle Jake and the Bell Handle," as well as fragmentary works.

1888   Crane enters the Hudson River Institute (Claverack College), Claverack, New York. Begins working for his brother, Townley Crane, in his Press Bureau at Asbury Park.

1890   Crane enrolls at Lafayette College; joins Delta Upsilon fraternity; fails his courses and drops out of Lafayette during Christmas vacation.

1891   Crane matriculates at Syracuse University on January 9; plays on the varsity baseball team; works on the newspapers; attends few classes; writes first draft of *Maggie*. Meets Hamlin Garland. Moves to New York City in the fall. His mother dies on December 7.

1892   Publishes five "Sullivan County Sketches" in the New York *Tribune* and one in *Cosmopolitan*.

1893   *Maggie: A Girl of the Streets* is privately printed. Through Garland meets William Dean Howells. Starts *The Red Badge of Courage*.

1894   Writes poems. Starts *George's Mother*. "An Experiment in Misery" and "An Experiment in Luxury" are printed. Abridged version of *The Red Badge of Courage* is published in newspapers by the Bacheller Syndicate.

1895   Goes West and to Mexico as syndicate feature writer from January to May; meets Willa Cather. *The Black Riders* and *The Red Badge of Courage* are published. Romantic attachment to Nellie Crouse. Crane now famous.

1896   Publishes *George's Mother, Maggie* (first commercial publication), *The Little Regiment, The Third Violet*, short stories, and poems. Dora Clark case. Meets Cora Taylor, five years his senior and proprietress of a house of assignation, in Jacksonville, Florida, where he is waiting to report on the Cuban insurrection.

1897   Shipwrecked on January 2 off the coast of Florida; publishes "The Open Boat," based on this incident. Covers Greco-Turkish War from April to May as correspondent for *New York Journal* and *Westminster Gazette*. Cora Taylor accompanies Crane as first woman war correspondent, signing her articles as "Imogene Carter." The Cranes (Cora as Mrs. Crane) settle in Oxted, Surrey. Meets Joseph Conrad.

1898   *The Open Boat and Other Tales of Adventure* published.
        Volunteers for Spanish-American War; rejected by
        Navy; hired as war correspondent for Pulitzer from
        April to November. First-rate dispatches and hero-
        ic comportment during period of involvement at
        Guantanamo, Cuzco, Las Guasimas, and San
        Juan Hill. Fired by Pulitzer; ill, returns to New
        York. Hired by Hearst; goes to Puerto Rico, then
        to Havana, and "disappears," spending his time
        writing and recuperating. Publication of "Death
        and the Child," "The Monster," "The Bride Comes
        to Yellow Sky," and "The Blue Hotel." Returns to
        New York in November.

1899   Publishes *War Is Kind*, a volume of poetry, *Active
        Service*, and *The Monster and Other Stories*. Returns to
        Cora; they live at Brede Manor, Sussex; lavish
        entertainment; writes continuously to meet enor-
        mous debts. Begins *The O'Ruddy*, a historical ro-
        mance completed by Robert Barr in 1903. At big
        Christmas week party, Crane suffers a severe tu-
        bercular hemorrhage.

1900   Dies of tuberculosis on June 5 in a sanitorium in
        Badenweiler, Germany. Buried in Hillside, New
        Jersey. *The Whilomville Stories*, *Wounds in the Rain*,
        Cuban sketches and stories, published posthu-
        mously.

1901   Cora returns to Jacksonville (d. 1910).

STEPHEN CRANE

Introduction

Stephen Crane's work has been described by H. G. Wells as "the first expression of the opening mind of a new period, or, at least, the early emphatic phase of a new initiative."[1] Indeed Crane's ideas, style, and approach to writing in his first novel, *Maggie: A Girl of the Streets* (1893), were so new that the manuscript was rejected by all the publishers to whom it was submitted, and eventually Crane paid for its printing out of his own pocket. Publishers did not want to invest money in what they considered a risky enterprise. Readers, in their opinion, would not accept Crane's bitter ironies and his true-to-life depictions of class warfare, all of which critics later called "the first dark flower of American Naturalism." The American public, or so the publishers believed, preferred to be entertained, to be nurtured on romantic love stories, to slip out of a humdrum world into one of beauty, mirth, and fantasy. Above all, it wanted morally redeeming plots: the villain had to be punished and the God-fearing waif rewarded. There were some writers of the time who recognized Crane's greatness. Hamlin Garland and William Dean Howells were fascinated by *Maggie*; they considered it a work of genius. Crane's vision was somber, tragic, but always authentic; his finely honed language, was bone-hard, incantatory, deeply sensual in its rhythmic patterns and auditory effects.

Crane's second novel, *The Red Badge of Courage: An Episode of the American Civil War*, earned him international fame for its story of a young soldier's struggle for self-knowledge. Crane's images, ranging from individual portraits to panoramic canvases, are unforgettable for their thickly daubed pigmentations and also for their smooth and velvety hues. Mythical in dimension, *The Red Badge of Courage* strikes powerfully into the readers' heart, as do some works of Melville and Hemingway, and a handful of the other greats of American literature. Writers as diverse as Joseph Conrad, Henry James, H. G. Wells, and later, Robert Frost, Ezra Pound, and Willa Cather have hailed Crane as one of the finest creative spirits of his time.

Crane wrote his novels, short stories, poems and journalistic dispatches rapidly and passionately, as if he knew from the very outset of his career that his time on earth would be only twenty-eight years. His poems, with their strong tonal qualities and bold visualizations convey not only a passion for life but also an unbridled rage against God. The Methodist minister's son repudiated the God he once had been taught to love. In *The Black Riders* Crane writes:

> Blustering god
> Stamping across the sky
> With loud swagger,
> I fear you not.

Crane's "War Is Kind" remains one of the most extraordinary antiwar poems of all time.

Crane's tales of adventure, of war, of New York City, and of the small towns in which he grew up, can be compared to those of Tolstoy, Chekhov, and other internationally known writers. The tales reveal the richness of Crane's intensely fertile imagination, his dry, controlled irony, and his protagonists' visceral drives to dig deeply into themselves and struggle with the world. Such diverse stories as "The Open Boat," "The Blue Hotel," "The Bride Comes to Yellow Sky," "The Upturned Face," "The Mystery of Heroism," "The Pace of Youth," and "The Monster," introduce the reader to a world where mood and atmosphere are taut and rhythms of the prose vibrate. A deeply *religious* note is implicit in these works: not one of organized religion, to be sure, but Crane's own mystical affinity to the universe in all of its moods, be they constructive or destructive. He frequently creates a mystical-religious atmosphere through sparkling and mat hues, harmonies and cacophonies, and also lulling or spasmodic rhythms. Crane has been called an impressionist because of the intensity of his verbal colorations, his sequences of image, and his optical mixings, which capture the impression of light and form at a given moment. Because of the precision of his representations, he has also been labeled a realist — sometimes even a naturalist. To these appellations one more might be added: he was an expressionist. Like Grunewald in the fifteenth century and Kokoschka in our time, Crane's work exhibits high emotion and exaggerated or distorted form. His ability to observe, absorb, and recreate what he intuited, saw, and felt in harsh, brutal images gave vividness and power to his writings. But he was also a symbolist in that every element of his writings — the flag, the skies, the water, the characters — may be viewed as an expression of an invisible, ineffable realm. Crane works through suggestion.

As a war correspondent during the Greco-Turkish War and the Spanish-American War, Crane's dispatches were always exciting, replete with humor, irony, and satire. Although he never feared negative criticism, he did yield at times to the pressures put on him by the yellow press. There was, however, nothing sham in his reportages. Even when enfeebled by malaria and tuberculosis or under such stressful conditions as shellfire, he endowed his writings with an inner energy all his own.

Like the Count de Lautréamont, Arthur Rimbaud, and other young men who gave profoundly of themselves in their writings, Crane transmuted into the world what gnawed so deeply at his vitals. Lautréamont died mysteriously at twenty-four and Rimbaud ended his literary career at twenty-one but each in his own way distilled his primal energies, loves, and hatreds into masterpieces that haunt the reader even today.

Always of universal impact, Crane's characters stalk the broad beds of eternity. Stark in their humanity, they are anguished in their search for an answer to life's cruelties. Crane's bold and brash metaphors and epithets hit their marks like bullets. His writings are provocative and sometimes jarring, but compassionate as well.

He was a rebel and a precursor of the creative spirits of the Lost Generation, the Beat Generation, and the Absurdists. As Joseph Conrad wrote: "his passage on this earth was like that of a horseman riding swiftly in the dawn of a day fated to be short and without sunshine."[2]

Part I

The Life

Virtues are, in the popular estimate, rather the exception than the rule. There is the man and his virtues. Men do what is called a good action, as some piece of courage or charity, much as they would pay a fine in expiation of daily non-appearance on parade. Their works are done as an apology or extenuation of their living in the world, — as invalids and the insane pay a high board. Their virtues are penances. I do not wish to expiate, but to live. My life is not an apology, but a life. It is for itself and not for spectacle.

— Ralph Waldo Emerson, "Self-Reliance"

1

The Story of His Life

Stephen Crane's career as a novelist, poet, and short story writer is indeed surprising when one considers his upbringing. The reading of fiction, except for the most anodyne type of works featuring virtuous people in pleasant surroundings, was strictly forbidden by his parents, who maintained an austere and religious home. Crane's father, Jonathan Townley, was a revivalist Methodist minister, who taught his family to fear divine retribution and the infernal pit into which all nonbelievers would be thrust. His mother, Mary Helen Peck, the daughter of a minister, was even more church-oriented than her husband, spending most of her time, when not caring for her eight children (six others did not survive), doing church work. Later she became a reporter of religious activities for various newspapers and an outspoken member of the Women's Christian Temperance Union, which considered smoking, drinking, and dancing sinful.

Born on November 1, 1871, in Newark, New Jersey, Stephen was a frail child who frequently suffered from colds and consequently did not attend school until he was seven. His older sister, Agnes, cared for him and instructed him in basic subjects since his mother was too busy with her many duties to give him the special attention he needed. When Agnes died at only twenty-eight, Stephen felt the loss of his beloved surrogate mother most keenly.

Reverend Crane worked long and arduously to

meet the needs of his parishioners, but he also was preoccupied with the financial problems of feeding his large family. This necessitated several moves to larger and more prosperous communities. The family went from Newark to Bloomington and then to Paterson, finally settling in Port Jervis, near Hartwood. Port Jervis had an ideal climate for young Stephen. This hilly region, intersecting New York, New Jersey, and Pennsylvania, with its many fields, ponds, and rivers helped to strengthen the ailing seven-year-old who loved the freedom of outdoor life. Years later, he immortalized this verdant terrain in his "Whilomville" tales.

It was at Port Jervis that Stephen first attended school. A bright student, he skipped two grades in six weeks, making up almost immediately for his late start. He was popular with friends and their families, his amiable and spirited ways endearing him to almost everyone. But this carefree and relatively happy time in the young boy's life came to a sudden halt with the death of his father in 1880. His mother moved first to a house in the outskirts of Newark and then, after Crane's bout with scarlet fever in 1882, to Asbury Park on the New Jersey Coast, where a daughter, Mary Helen Hamilton, taught art, and a son, Jonathan Townley, ran a news-reporting agency in the summer months for the New York *Tribune*. Jonathan already employed his brother Wilbur, and eventually would employ his mother and his youngest brother, Stephen.

Crane seemed to thrive in his new surroundings. Hiking, fishing, and swimming brought him intense joy. He attended the local school and, entertaining thoughts of becoming a professional baseball player, joined the Asbury Park baseball team. Later, he enrolled at the Pennington Seminary in New Jersey, where his father had been principal for ten years prior to the Civil War.

Even before he could read, Crane enjoyed looking

at the black letters written or imprinted on white pages. Their configurations and designs fascinated him. When older, he used to spend periods of time toying with words, as one plays games, inventing new verbs and nouns, delighting in their onomatopoeic effects, their clang appeal, their rhythms — and sensuality. Crane's earliest extant manuscript, "Uncle Jake and the Bell-Handle" (1885) — a staightforward and simple tale — is already stamped by what will become the characteristics of his prose: an intense feeling for nature in all of its manifestations, a rich palette of colors that reflect emotional conditions, and vivid dialogue, marked by various regional accents.

Crane as a young boy also enjoyed mock battles and war games. His play-acting depictions of colorful uniforms and flags (red and blue were always his favorite colors) excited him, as did the conflagration of clashing forces and enemy attacks. Struggle must have ignited a spark within him that later took on creative power. He had been taught to take pride in his ancestry, and his namesake, the grandson of still another Stephen Crane, a seventeenth-century colonizer from England or Wales, had been President of the Colonial Assemblies. Other descendants had fought with distinction in the army and navy during the Revolutionary War. That he should ask his mother to send him to the quasimilitary Hudson River Institute in Claverack New York was not surprising.

The strict interdictions and religious discipline under which Crane had lived during his childhood caused him fears and anxieties which he sought to overcome in his years as a Claverack student (1888–90). Rebelling against the restrictions imposed upon him by his parents, he smoked incessantly (with deleterious effects on his lungs), drank excessive amounts of beer, gambled, swore, danced, played pool and poker, and often went to the theater. As for sex, Reverend Crane had never spoken out or written against it in his works: *The Right Way* (1853), *Arts of Intoxication* (1870), and *Popular Amusements* (1869). How could he, the father of fourteen children, depict sex as an evil? He did, however, stress the sanctity of married life and spoke of the importance of the home. His undue emphasis on a tightly knit cell-like existence, however, may have caused Crane to go to such extremes as frequenting prostitutes and eventually settling down in 1896 with the twice-married Cora Taylor Howorth, proprietress of a house of assignation in Jacksonville.

Claverack was not only a quasimilitary school but also, much to Crane's delight, it was coeducational. In the first semester, he had crushes on three different girls. He preferred drinking, gambling, and baseball and other sports to mathematics and science, but he did enjoy history and literature, especially the Greek and Roman classics. He also was an inveterate reader of nineteenth-century English and American novels and poetry. He sang tenor in the choir of the Methodist Church in Claverack and offered his services pumping the organ at the college—not without premeditation, since he would be allowed to sit out what he considered interminable sermons. Although Crane was aware of having learned little at Claverack, he later considered those rough-and-tumble school years as the happiest in his life.[1]

In 1890 he transferred to Lafayette College in Easton, Pennsylvania. Obsessed with fear over the cruelties he had heard took place during the hazing period, he decided (wisely as it turned out) to keep with him at all times a loaded revolver, which he had purchased from a Wyoming cowboy for five dollars. When the upper classmen entered his room to put him through their harsh disciplines, Crane was so shaken that as he reached for his revolver, it dropped to the floor. His attackers, stunned to see the revolver, stopped in their tracks, convinced that this young man was strong, proud, and wild. Crane was never again troubled by them.

Academically, Crane was no more successful at Lafayette than he had been at Claverack. He attended very few of his classes and continued drinking, gambling, boxing, and playing baseball. As before he was still an avid reader and profoundly impressed with Tolstoy's *Sebastopol* and Flaubert's *Madame Bovary*. By the end of the semester, it was suggested that he leave school.

In January of 1891 Crane enrolled at Syracuse University where he fared no better, leaving after one semester for the same reasons as before. Fun, rather than scholarship was his goal. But most significant for him was his writing of the initial draft of what was to become his first major novel, *Maggie: A Girl of the Streets*. Despite his failing grades, people were attracted to this slim five-foot-six-inch young man, whose serious air and exciting conversation were impressive. He was handsome: "with [his] finely chiseled but rather delicate features and a large head covered with a luxuriant growth of light hair, which falls in careless disorder over a high forehead. The blue eyes which look out from beneath have a suggestion of weariness and even of sadness in them when the brain behind is passive, but when it is alert and active, as in interesting conversation, they light up and flash with sparkling animation. His eyes are a good index of his temperament."[2]

Crane's mother was concerned—understandably so—over her son's dismissal from Syracuse University. But when he told her of his intention to become a writer, she agreed to his plans immediately. At least he would do *something* besides gamble, drink, smoke, and participate in sports. But in actuality, Crane had already had some of his tales published in the Syracuse University *Herald* ("The King's Favor") and in the New York *Tribune* ("Great Bugs at Onondaga").

August 17, 1891 was to be a memorable date for

Crane. He attended Hamlin Garland's lecture on William Dean Howells and wrote it up for the *Tribune*.[3] Garland (1860–1940), a protégé of Howells', was already an important literary figure. Born in Wisconsin, he was raised in the midwestern farmlands, which he commemorated in such tales, novels, autobiography, and essays as *Main-travelled Roads* (1891), *A Little Norsk* (1892), and *Jason Edwards: An Average Man* (1892). His realistic depictions of the futile and difficult lives of farmers both shocked and impressed many readers of his day with their truthfulness, and outspoken and graphic descriptions. A literary *veritist*, he was also an advocate of the single-tax doctrine and a supporter of the Populist party.

The Ohio-born William Dean Howells (1837–1920) was, of course, one of the outstanding critics, novelists, and editors of his time. An extensive traveler—appointed consul to Venice in 1861—his early writings, moralistic comedies of manners (*The Wedding Journey* published in 1872 and *The Lady of Aroostook* in 1879), brought him only faint praise.

He won fame, though, when he turned toward realism with such novels as *A Modern Instance* (1882), *The Rise of Silas Lapham* (1885), and *Indian Summer* (1886). His essays on Tolstoy, Zola, and Ibsen fashioned American taste, and inspired writers such as Twain, Garland, and Veblen, who were increasingly tormented by the social conflict and suffering brought about by industrialization. Howells blamed America's decay on the rule of competitive capitalism. A mitigated form of socialism was his answer to life's hardships, which he dramatized in such novels as *A Hazard of New Fortunes* (1890) and *An Imperative Duty* (1893). Howells was uncompromising in recounting the infernal squalor and human degradation of New York's Bowery. He likewise did not temper his attacks against the wealthy who doled out their riches to the poor, or against the middle class's ambivalent attitudes toward the destitute. Howells advocated a type of writing that would observe life as it is and speak out the plain truth. "[T]his truth given, the book *cannot* be wicked and cannot be weak; and without it all graces of style and feats of invention and cunning of construction are so many superfluities of naughtiness."[4]

Garland and Howells were to play a decisive role in Crane's growth as a novelist and teller of tales. Realism and authenticity, however, were not the only factors of import to Crane during the summer of 1891. He met and fell in love with Helen Trent, a tall, beautiful contralto who sang at charity concerts in the Bowery, which she described as "a slum as vile as anything in Paris or in Munich." Tantalized by her grace and winning nature, he was smitten with her. [5]

Although Crane was destitute most of the time, barely having enough to eat, his family came to his help when he needed it. He could count on his brother, who ran the news agency for the *Tribune*, and on another brother, Judge William Howe Crane. William had opened a law office at Port Jervis in 1882 and owned a total of 3,500 acres of land next to the elegant Hartwood Club, of which he was president. Crane vacationed in magnificent Hartwood Park in Sullivan County with his parents in 1879 and later spent many a summer and winter holiday at Port Jervis swimming, riding horseback and camping.

"Sullivan County Sketches" (1891–96), which commemorates this region, is not one of Crane's finest works, but it reveals him to be an outstanding spinner of yarns. His themes of hunting, fishing, and camping are slight to be sure, but the suspense, verity, and irony of some of these tales and fables are unforgettable.

Like Poe, Crane knows how to present a world of imponderables that arouses a sense of mystery and wonderment in the reader.

"Four Men in a Cave" (July 3, 1892), for example, tells the story of a young man and three of his friends, who are determined to investigate a remote cave in the Hartwood area. On a moonlit night, the men make their way to this subterranean vault. As they penetrate the inner recesses of this black maw, they see "a floor of damp clay and pebbles, the walls slimy, green-mossed and dripping." The atmosphere grows increasingly frightening, an effect Crane achieves, in large part, through his enchanting use of alliteration — "they slid down the slippery, slimy floor of the passage" — which amplifies the sounds and recreates the rhythm of the men's descent. In the middle of an opening, they see "A great gray stone, cut squarely, like an altar" and above "burned three candles in swaying tin cups hung from the ceiling." Near it stands a man, clasping a book in his hands, who "fixed glinting, fiery eyes upon the heap of them and remained motionless." Unsure whether they are looking at a vampire, a ghoul, or an Aztec witch doctor, the intruders are both fascinated and terrified. When they spy two skeletal hounds next to this priest-like individual, they run from the cave, fearing for their lives. Later they learn that this strange man was a former gambler who had gone mad after having lost everything he had, even his wife whom he cherished.[6]

The opening of "Killing His Bear" (July 31, 1892) arouses all the reader's senses, as tones ring out and visual images appear and then fade in a rhythmic interchange of cinematic-like close-ups and distant shots. "In a field of snow some green pines huddled together and sang in quavers as the wind whirled among the gullies and ridges. Icicles dangled from the trees' beards, and fine dusts of snow lay upon their brows. On the ridge-top a dismal choir of hemlocks crooned over one that had fallen. The dying sun created a dim purple and flame-colored tumult on the horizon's edge and then sank until level crimson beams struck the trees. As the red rays retreated, armies of shadows stole forward. A gray, ponderous stillness came heavily in the steps of the sun. A little man stood under the quavering pines." Now that Crane has set the stage, he creates further excitement and awe by emphasizing the endless silence. "The earth faded to nothing. Only space and the game, the aim and the hunter. Mad emotions, powerful to rock worlds, hurled through the little man, but did not shake his tiniest nerve." As the bear—hugely massive—turns on the hunter, a shot rings out. The man thrills at his achievements; he sees the dying animal and begins waving "his hat as if he were leading the cheering of thousands. He ran up and kicked the ribs of the bear. Upon his face was the smile of the successful lover." Here Crane, aroused by the hunter's cruelty, sides with the animal.

Crane handles language in such a way that it becomes a powerful weapon capable of conveying an image in all of its nuances. The coldness of the landscape and the stillness of the atmosphere are evoked stunningly by Crane's use of "primitive" word associations and his blending of visual, tactile, and olfactory sensations.

It was at this juncture—in 1892—that Crane gave up the "clever Rudyard Kipling style." Had he continued in this vein, he wrote, "the road might have been shorter, but, ah, it wouldn't be the true road." Crane was now certain that he wanted to emulate Howells and Garland, becoming "involved in the beautiful war between those who say that art is man's substitute for nature and we are the most successful in art when we approach the nearest to nature and truth."

Crane's avowed admiration for Garland and Howells did not do away with Kipling's powerful hold upon him—though he did not acknowledge Kipling's influence. It is well to recall that Kipling was a master at creating fervent and majestic moods, who used great simplicity and vigor when he depicted character. Although his prose was at times disfigured by a staccato style, his *Plain Tales* (1887), published before he was twenty-four, was supremely skillful. Crane was impressed by the freshness and inventiveness of Kipling's images, the magic of his exuberance, and the vitality and raciness of his dialogue. What Crane found distasteful and rejected overtly, however, was Kipling's pomposity, his imperialistic notions of the white man's burden, and his mannered tricks.

The summer of 1892, when Crane gave up the Kipling style, was marked by yet another significant event. While working for the *New York Tribune* at Asbury Park, he met Lily Brandon Munroe at the elegant Lake Avenue Hotel. She was beautiful and charming, and the two spent long hours strolling along the boardwalk. Lily inspired him to write "The Pace of Youth." Crane saw her the following winter.[7] Lily considered him scrawny and not at all handsome, but she did love him and might have agreed to be his wife, had she not been married. Persisting in his intoxication, Crane still wrote her passionate letters two years after they had met.[8] Lily fulfilled Crane's needs for warmth, gentleness, and understanding, which allowed him eventually to speak the language of his feelings in *The Third Violet*, a novel that commemorates their romance.

Meanwhile, Crane was reworking his novel, *Maggie*, and was writing articles filled with Asbury Park shore news for the *Tribune*: "On the New Jersey Coast," "Summer Dwellers at Asbury Park and their Doings," "On the Boardwalk." His first sketch of New York City, "The Broken-Down Van," appeared in 1892, initiating a series he was to write about New York. Crane was now spending his days and nights on the Bowery, trying to experience the world of the poor and the deprived. He wanted to free himself from the "nicely laundered lives" of his relatives and friends at Port Jervis and

Asbury Park; he looked upon their world as superficial and egotistic. He sought to experience life in the raw, to know it *plain.*

Since Crane's first meeting with Garland, he had taken Garland's advice that to understand hard times one had to live them. Crane joined the throngs of people who suffered cold and wetness, who huddled together in front of shelters and soup kitchens, waiting patiently for handouts. During the February blizzard of 1894, Crane and an illustrator friend left their overcoats at home and donned rags and wornout shoes to join the bread lines. Only by rubbing shoulders with society's pariahs did Crane feel he would be able to convey authentically this world to his readers. Unfortunately his health was weakened. He suffered from a dry, hacking cough, made worse by inadequate food. But Crane was nevertheless right: his stories "An Experiment in Misery" and "Men in the Storm" are indeed masterpieces of this genre.[9]

Frequently Crane begins his narratives by setting the stage. "An Experiment in Misery" illustrates this: "It was late at night, and a fine rain was swirling softly down, causing the pavements to glisten with hue of steel and blue and yellow in the rays of the innumerable lights." The interweaving of soft and harsh tonalities points up the stressful suffering and pain of the characters, whose dismal lives Crane is about to depict. A young man is described walking down the street, hands in his pockets, looking for a shelter for the night. As he reaches City Hall Park, he is overwhelmed by a feeling of rejection. He hears the cat calls hurled at him — bum, hobo, and other epithets — making him feel not only the butt of ridicule but an exile from humanity. Continuing up to Park Row, then to Chatham Square, he meets others like him, and his sense of loneliness diminishes. He stops in front of a saloon that offers free hot soup with a beer. He goes in. Sipping the broth, he feels warmth invade his body. As he looks around, he sees a drunken man so strangely dressed that he reminds him of an "assassin steeped in crime." This would-be criminal offers to take him to a lodging house for three pennies. Out in the cold again, the two walk in silence, then enter a building through a long dark corridor. The lodging house is tightly packed with cots and lockers that remind the young man of "tombstones"; the men lie about "in death-like silence or heaving and snoring with tremendous effort, like stabbed fish." He shivers at this sight, lies down on a cot and thinks about the tragedy of these lives. The men talk of pain in their sleep and the gloominess of their agonized wails prevents the lad from sleeping. He observes the sadness of those near him, "carving biographies for these men from his meager experience." The following morning he leaves, entering a quite different neighborhood where people wear sumptuous garments. An infinite gap separates them from those of the night before. Crane's compassion for the outcasts of society is evident, but his avoidance of sentimentality only increases the story's stark effect.

In "Men in the Storm," Crane conveys moments of intense agitation while remaining at a distance from the events he is describing. The detachment achieved through this technique helps Crane to phrase his sentences with dexterity. Crane frames the sequences in "The Men in the Storm" as Stieglitz does his photographs: focusing upon, then capturing and encapsulating, the nuances of black-and-white shadings. Stieglitz sees beyond this interplay of light and dark colors when evoking atmosphere, emotion, and the corrosive sense of solitude that dominates the lives of each of the men in the picture. Crane's writing often has symbolic overtones; each character is imprisoned, body and mind, by his class and his poverty, his alienation caused by an inability to communicate with his fellow man: "The sidewalk soon became completely blocked by the bodies of the men. They pressed close to one another like sheep in a winter's gale, keeping one another warm by the heat of their bodies. The snow came down upon this compressed group of men until, directly from above, it might have appeared like a heap of snow-covered merchandise, if it were not for the fact that the crowd swayed gently with a unanimous rhythmical motion." The snow thickens, the cold intensifies, and the wind swirls as "great clouds of snow" sweep through the streets. Crane's delineations are so vivid that one can feel, taste, absorb, inhale the cold wetness of the snow as it descends, cutting each individual off from the real world, forcing him back into his remote, bleak solitude. The poor wait, pushing and shoving, for the doors of the soup kitchens, bakeries, and saloons to open. This grim and harrowing scene, Crane suggested, had a "wondrous undereffect, indefinable and mystic, as if there was some kind of humor in this catastrophe, in this situation in a night of snow-laden winds." Crane frequently questioned, not without irony: if God is all merciful, how could such misery exist in a world that he created?

Like Frank Norris (1870–1902), the author of *Mc-Teague*, Crane's writings now centered on the lives of the proletariat. Both were decisively influenced by Emile Zola's (1840–1902) naturalism. Zola had written in *The Experimental Novel*: "In short, we must operate with characters, passions, human and social data as the chemist and the physicist work on inert bodies, as the geologist works on living bodies." Zola believed that great art had to deal with society's momentous changes and upheavals as he did in his series of novels, *The Rougon-Macquart*. Reconciling his romantic individualism and idealism to his increasing commitment to realism, Zola demanded that writers analyze documents of all types and use the information in their novels, thus transforming fiction

by scientific methodology into physiological and sociological realism.

Although not a determinist, Crane did take into
account an individual's environment, agreeing that it
played a role in human development. Crane believed,
however, that other vagaries of fate, such as an "indifferent" and frequently "hostile" nature, were also enor-
mously significant. Like Zola, he sought to get to the
root of problems and to describe honestly what he saw.
He rejected both Kipling's mannerisms and the many-
faceted prose that Henry James used to probe the infinite nuances of the psyche. Instead, Crane held up a
mirror to nature and depicted the world as he saw it,
without mercy and often brutally. Enriched by experience, he felt that he was ready to present to the American reader the savage world around him. *Maggie*, his
first masterpiece, was in the offing.

Crane began his second novel dealing with slum
life, *George's Mother*, in 1894, prior to *Maggie's* publication, but it was not completed before the publication of
The Red Badge of Courage in 1895, the year in which he
met and fell in love with Nellie Crouse.[10] Their romance was only of an epistolary nature, however, con-
sisting of seven letters dealing for the most part with
Crane's literary prospects, ideas, and goals.[11] His last
letter to Nellie Crouse concludes on a note of despair:
"If there is a joy of living, I can't find it. The future?
The future is blue with obligations — new trials — conflicts. It was a rare old wine the gods brewed *for mortals*.
Flagons of despair."[12]

Not all of Crane's associations with women were on
a high intellectual level. His need for low life was always
present. Moreover, he was beginning a new set of articles, similar to his *New York Press* series, called "Midnight Sketches" (1893–94), which would include about
twenty gripping depictions of street life. To write about
vices and miseries not yet touched upon by other jour-

nalists would also, he hoped, increase the sales of the newspapers for which he wrote and thus also his own fame.

Prostitution was now one of Crane's themes, a subject on which he was by no means unknowledge-able. What many people were not aware of was his often misplaced generosity. When Doris Watt com-plained that she was destitute and asked Crane for fifty dollars, he gave it to her though he could ill afford it. After he received another demand for money, this time for one-hundred-and-fifty dollars, he again acquiesced. Nothing more is known of the affair.[13]

The most publicized of his relationships with pros-titutes was the one with Dora Clark. The facts are known, but whether the entire event was a hoax or a staged performance to call attention to Crane's work or to the corruption of the police force is clouded in mys-tery. Was Crane working with Theodore Roosevelt, then President of the Board of Police Commissioners, who was attempting to eradicate moral and social in-fractions in his law enforcement department? We know Roosevelt admired Crane. When Crane sent him an inscribed copy of *George's Mother*, he requested one of *The Red Badge of Courage*. But it was after reading *Maggie* first that Roosevelt asked Crane to come to his office.

The facts in the Dora Clark case are still unclear. Crane seemingly had made an appointment to meet some "chorus girls" one of whom was Dora Clark. Clark was a streetwalker with a few aliases, who had been arrested several times for soliciting at the Turkish Smoking Parlors on West Twenty-ninth Street during September of 1896. Crane wanted to interview the women for his articles — studies of various New York City districts — to be published in Hearst's *Journal* (Sep-tember 20) and in *Book News*. After obtaining the neces-sary information, he went with Dora Clark and two other "chorus girls" to the Broadway Garden. At two o'clock in the morning, Crane called an end to the interviews, walked to Broadway and Thirty-first Street, accompanying one of the women to her uptown trolley across the street and leaving Dora Clark and the others standing on the corner. Moments later, a detective attempted to arrest the women. Crane realized instantly that they were being framed, and spoke out in their defense. The "chorus girl" became hysterical when the policeman gripped her arm and shrieked out that Crane was her husband. He confirmed the statement and she was freed. Dora Clark, however, was held overnight in a cell.

According to newspaper reports, Crane was outraged by this injustice. He was determined to testify at Dora Clark's trial, although he was warned not to do so by the kindhearted Sergeant McDermott and by Roosevelt and Garland as well. The scandal would not help his reputation, they told him; it would only bring him further condemnation. Garland told Crane he would do better to return to his brother's farm in Sullivan County and get back his color. But Crane listened to no one and eventually testified at the trial. "I know this girl to be innocent," Crane had said to Garland.[14]

During the trial, Dora Clark claimed she had been arrested on prior occasions because she refused the advances of policemen and that she had been wrongly accused this time as well. Crane was praised in the Hearst *Journal* for his courage in protecting an innocent person and for rising above the many aspersions leveled at him. After Dora Clark's release, the police force promised not to harass Crane or the plaintiff. When they reneged on their word Crane wrote "Notes about Prostitutes" and "A Blackguard as a Police Officer," which argued that the right to arrest is the most dangerous power that society can give anyone. Neither Crane's testimony nor his articles endeared him to the police force. Roosevelt was also displeased and cut short his relations with Crane.

There were other seedy relationships, more mysterious perhaps than the Dora Clark affair but less damaging to Crane's reputation. Amy Leslie, drama critic for the *Chicago News* and former actress, stated she had lent the author eight-hundred dollars and wanted the money back. To prevent a law suit, Crane complied.

Crane's articles dealt not only with police corruption and prostitution but also with dope addiction. In "Opium's Varied Dreams," written for the *New York Sun* (May 17, 1896), he reported on Chinatown, with its tortuous and cluttered streets and its dismal dens, pipes, lamps, and yen-hocks where the opium addict found his drug. Some time later, when Crane mentioned to an acquaintance that he had tried opium to see what it was really like, the rumor spread that he had fallen victim to this vice.[15]

Crane had begun writing his fourth novel in 1895: *The Third Violet*, which he described as "really the history of the love of one of the younger and brilliant American artists for an heiress of the ancient New York family kind." Love stories, however, were not Crane's forte, and this novel did not breathe much life.[16] He was out of his milieu: "New York was essentially his inspiration, the New York of suffering and baffled and beaten life, of inarticulate or blasphemous life; and away from it he was not at home, with any theme, or any sort of character," Howells had written, and he was right.[17]

After *The Red Badge of Courage* and several short stories dealing with the military, Crane developed an obsession with participating in a war, or at least seeing some fighting. He achieved his goal rather circuitously. Having received seven-hundred dollars in gold from Irving Bacheller to report on the Cuban rebellion, he left for Jacksonville, Florida in November of 1896, without having had time to notify his family or friends of his departure. He waited until January for a filibustering ship to take him to Cuba. Although he did not enjoy the waiting period, he found Jacksonville, a city of about twenty-eight thousand people, awash with newsmen, adventurers, and all types of people wanting to get to Cuba for one reason or another. Hotels, bars, and gambling dens were filled to capacity, as were the opera houses, waterfront saloons, and brothels.[18]

Soon after Crane's arrival, he went to the Hotel de Dream where he met its hostess, the goldenhaired Cora Taylor (Howorth Murphy Stewart). "Miss Cora," as she was called, directed a "Class A" house of assignation, which was frequented only by the *right* people. She had a certain elegance of her own, having come from a refined Boston family. Her father, John Howorth, had been a painter; her grandfather, George Howorth, had run a Boston art gallery. Cora was a fighter and rebelled against what she considered an overly refined and traditional heritage. She married a man named Thomas Murphy, divorced him, married Captain Donald W. Stewart, a much-decorated soldier of the empire, and then left him when he went overseas for colonial service. Stewart refused to give her a divorce, which led Cora to settle in Jacksonville and begin a new trade. Intelligent, witty, and attractive, she impressed Crane with both her physical and intellectual gifts. Since she was well read, they discussed literature and a host of other topics. After their first meeting, Crane gave her a copy of *George's Mother*, which he inscribed: "To an unnamed sweetheart." In a note to her he wrote a sentence that reflects his tragic view of life: "brevity is an element that enters importantly into all pleasures of life, and this is what makes pleasure sad; and so there is no pleasure but sadness."[19]

Cora fell completely and passionately in love, and her love was reciprocated, at least as much as was possible for a wandering man like Crane. While waiting for a ship to take him to Cuba, he saw Cora frequently. He finally sailed from Jacksonville to Cuba on the ill-fated Commodore, which was carrying weapons from the

United States to the Cuban insurrectionists fighting against Spain. The vessel sank about fifteen miles from shore. Most of the crew, as well as Crane, were able to escape in life boats and rafts and made it to Daytona Beach. Crane remained overnight in a home near the Halifax River. Cora, frantic and without worrying about the high cost, wired him to hire a special locomotive back to Jacksonville. When it came to matters of the heart, this largesse was characteristic.[20]

After a week's rest in Jacksonville, Crane regained his strength and was ready to set out again for Cuba. The revenue cutters were increasingly vigorous in enforcing America's neutrality, however, and it was impossible for Crane to find a vessel that was going to Cuba. Crane felt a genuine need to be in the thick of *real* action; adventure and excitement stimulated him and were an inspiration to his writing. He decided, therefore, to go to Greece, where a war with the Turks was imminent. Cora, not wanting to remain behind, sold the Hotel de Dream and wound up her affairs in Jacksonville; the first woman war correspondent was born.

Reaching London on March 29, 1897, Crane visited his English publisher, Heinemann Ltd, and met the American novelist and journalist, Harold Frederic, who had written a glorious review of *The Red Badge of Courage*. Crane also was introduced to Richard Harding Davis, a reporter for the London *Times*, who was to cover the war in Greece. En route to his destination, Crane visited Paris and saw the sights including Notre Dame with its "altars." He told a friend, Sandford (Arnold) Bennett, "I can't stand that nonsense."[21]

The causes of the Greco-Turkish War are relatively uncomplicated. Bloodshed and rebellion had plagued Crete for twelve years following in 1878 the Congress of Berlin's refusal of the island's request for independence from its Turkish rulers. Unprepared for such a struggle, the Greeks came to the aid of the Cretans, but then suffered defeat. Crane, there during the struggle, was not as objective as were the British and French newspapermen. His reports were slanted, sentimentalizing the patriotic heroism of the Greeks in "Greeks Cannot be Curbed," while also indulging his proclivity for idealizing war as virile and virtuous.

Crane's ultimate goal was achieved as he witnessed the Yanina campaign in April of 1897 and the second of three battles at Velestino in May.[22] He left the country shortly thereafter, enriched by the experience that was to serve as background for his novel *Active Service*.[23]

Crane, who had suffered a bout of dysentery returned to England after Cora, with a Greek dog and two Greek servants for the elegant house they had rented. Typical of both Crane and Cora, they lived well beyond their means. Crane found it necessary to work at a furious pace. He completed *Active Service* in January, 1899, and wrote some short stories, among them, "The Blue Hotel," and "Death and the Child." They had settled in Ravensbrook, England and led an active social life as husband and wife. (There is, however, no legal proof of their marriage, Cora having been unable to obtain a divorce from her second husband.) Perhaps to please his neighbors, with whom he later became friendly, Crane accepted an invitation to speak at the Socialist Fabian Society, even though he did not enjoy public speaking. His theme was "flag waving." Ford Madox Hueffer, later known as Ford Madox Ford, was present at the lecture and was taken aback by what he considered to be Crane's arrogance. Later, when he came to know Crane better, they became good friends. Ford even "revered" him; there was, he wrote, "something of the supernatural" in this "Apollo with starry eyes."[24]

Crane became friendly with other writers as well, among them Edmund Gosse and Joseph Conrad. Conrad, whom Crane met in 1897, once remarked: "What I discovered very early in our acquaintance was that Crane had not the face of a lucky man. It was the smile of a man who knows that his time will not be long on this earth."[25] Crane responded to Conrad's warmth and understanding and was also deeply impressed by his work, particularly *The Nigger of the 'Narcissus.'* Crane wrote, "The simple treatment of the death of Waite [sic] is too good, too terrible. I wanted to forget it at once. It caught me very hard. I felt ill over that red thread lining from the corner of the man's mouth to his chin. It was frightful with the weight of a real and present death. By such small means does the real writer suddenly flash out in the sky above those who are always doing rather well."[26]

H. G. Wells also became a close friend. Harold Frederic, a journalist and novelist, wrote about "The Open Boat" in the *New York Times*: "The genius of this young son of America is being keenly felt here [in London] . . . . No living English prose-writer of his years approaches his wonderful gift of original and penetrating observation, while no writer of English is today prouder of being an American."[27] The Frederics were living in Ireland at the time, and to visit them, the Cranes took the Scotch Express. In his article, "The Scotch Express," for *McLure's Magazine* (1899), Crane described the countryside, the hills and dales, the train, its engineer, the road beds, and the speed of the train. He was entranced by the Irish, though he did not hold their writers of the nineties in high esteem—except for Yeats.[28]

Writing was Crane's daily fare: articles such as "Fresh Bits of Gossip on European Affairs" (*New York Press*, 1897) and "London Impressions" for Frank Harris; contributions to *Saturday Review*; short stories such as "Flanagan and His Short Filibustering Adventure" for the *Illustrated London News*; "The Monster," "Death and the Child," and so on. Along with Whistler, James, and Conrad, Crane was much admired by the British; he was enjoying his fame and the British were enjoying the refreshing young American.

Crane could never stay in one place for any great length of time. When he heard that the American battleship, the Maine, had been blown up in Havana Harbor on February 15, his thoughts returned to his homeland, to adventure, and to war. President McKinley's address on April 11, 1898, asserting Cuba's independence from Spain was a virtual declaration of war, which filled Crane with excitement. He was ready to leave, but did not have the funds to get to the United States. Conrad, who saw Crane's "white-faced excitement" at the thought of leaving, lent him some money, though he could ill afford it. Later, however, Conrad felt remorse, believing he had contributed to the severe deterioration of Crane's health. He learned in time that he was not the only one who had lent Crane money; other friends as well as government agencies had done the same. "I was not the only blind agent of the fate that had him in her grip! Nothing could have held him back. HE WAS READY TO SWIM THE OCEAN."[29]

Reaching New York, Crane went directly to the offices of the United States Navy and tried to enlist as a seaman. Much to his disappointment, he was not accepted for health reasons. On April 23, 1898, he accepted Joseph Pulitzer's offer to be Cuban war correspondent for the *New York World*. Before his departure he made a trip to Washington to see the woman who still meant so much to him, Lily Brandon Munroe.

Events were moving rapidly. Spain declared war on the United States on April 24; the United States affirmed the fact that a state of war against Spain had existed since the twenty-first of the same month. Crane's new port of call was Key West; he wrote an account of the capture of a Spanish vessel in the harbor

there in "The Terrible Captain of the Captured Pana-
ma." The "rocking-chair" period of the war, as it was
called, followed. Generals and military men remained
in Tampa, surveying the situation from land.

On April 29, no longer willing to stand the inac-
tivity and aided by well-placed friends, Crane left for
Mariel, west of Havana, on the *New York World*'s tug-
boat, the *Triton*. He then boarded the *New York*, thirty-
five miles west of Havana, and reported on the bom-
bardment of Matanzas in his dispatch, "Sampson
Inspects the Harbor at Mariel." Continuing on to
Canabas, he witnessed a second naval engagement.
The American soldiers who landed in Cuba did not
fare well; three quarters of Colonel Roosevelt's Rough
Riders were struck down by malaria, which was called
the Cuban disease. By July, five-thousand soldiers of
the Fifth Army Corps also had become ill. The situation was growing precarious.[30]

Crane also succumbed to illness, but even though
fevers plagued him, he traveled with other correspondents around the area on dispatch boats, looking for
scoops on military movements and changing tugboats
whenever it meant getting closer to action. After writing "With the Blockade on the Cuban Coast" (May 7)
and other reportages, he returned to Key West and
Tampa. Finally, along with other reporters, he boarded
the tug, *Three Friends*, and sailed to Haiti, where he
experienced exciting adventures later recounted in his
semi-fictionalized "War Memories" (1899). Moving on
to San Domingo, he learned that the French and Ger-
man merchants on the island sided with the Spanish.
He sent dispatches such as "Narrow Escape of the *Three
Friends*," which stirred the hearts of his New York readers. His desire to see more action remained unfulfilled;
he saw only navy skirmishes, and very few of these.
Meanwhile, Crane traveled in whatever tugs were
available, nearing the coast of Santiago on the way to

Jamaica and circling around the island of Cuba in an attempt to ferret out the Spanish fleet. He occupied his time writing, playing poker, chatting, and telling tall tales.

Hearst, Pulitzer, and Bennett were not pleased with their journalists. They demanded more exciting news, ordering the correspondents to exaggerate events and inflate their importance. Crane did not like to agitate the American public by distorting the truth, but he sometimes yielded to the yellow journalism formula. At other times he satirized it, as in the dispatch, "The Majestic Lie," a kind of confession, in which he remarked: "We told them this and we told them that, and I warrant you our screaming sounded like the noise of a lot of sea birds settling for the night among the black crags."[31]

The landing of the American Marines on June tenth at Guantánamo Bay changed the pace of the war. Crane and the other journalists accompanying the American fighting force thought it "rather comic" that there was no firing that first night. The following day, however, the situation changed. "We lay on our bellies; it was no longer comic . . . feeling the hot hiss of the bullets trying to cut my hair. For the moment I was no longer a cynic. I was a child who, in a fit of ignorance, had jumped into the vat of war."[32] The firing continued. Someone next to Crane was killed, and there were a number of casualities. The entire incident was captured in Crane's poignant short story, "The Upturned Face."

Richard Harding Davis, a correspondent with whom Crane had spent much time, wrote that the American author was "the coolest man, whether army officer or civilian, that I saw under fire at any time during the war." An incident relating to Crane's heroism was recorded in the London *Daily Chronicle*. During the Cuzco Hill skirmish, Crane was close enough to an

American company that had been surrounded by
Spaniards to see that the soldiers had run out of water
in the 108 degree temperature. He wanted to bring the
soldiers water, but to do so required climbing a high,
steep hill in an area that was being shelled by the enemy. "Yet Stephen Crane never hesitated. Collecting
about a dozen big bottles, he retired to the rear, filled
them, and turned to climb the hill again—his little
person festooned with bottles," wrote the reporter who
saw the incident. "When he reached the fightingline he
dropped exhausted, and this gave rise to the report that
he had been shot. Happily, it was not true. The soldiers
were too busy to cheer him at the moment, but they
repaid him afterwards with their warmest admiration.
That was only one of the occasions on which he showed
his genuine pluck." According to this reporter and
friends of Crane, he did not look his age: "with his
fragile physique and shy and sensitive disposition, he
was the last man who might be expected to figure in the
storm and stress of battle. Yet 'Little Stevey'—as his
friends and colleagues delighted to call him—was pos-
sessed of the highest and truest courage, the courage of
the man of keen imagination and he proved it on more
than one stricken field."[33]

But Crane's health was deteriorating. His malaria
became increasingly serious, and some critics, Beer
and Berryman, believe that his high fever often caused
him to hallucinate. The vivid imagery of his dispatches
underscored the vicious nature of the fighting. His
gripping descriptions of Americans on their guerrilla
hunts, flushing the enemy out with shells and then
cutting them down, and his statement that war was "a
grim and frightful field sport" were not received well by
all readers. Forced to take quinine for his malaria,
Crane could digest virtually no food. He lived on coffee, cigarettes, alcohol, and fruit. Still, he pursued his
task, racing with the soldiers during skirmishes and

battles and also helping the wounded behind the lines. He was fighting a double battle: trying to remain alive and also attempting to complete his reports.

Crane's death wish was probably quite acute at that time; he not only simply disregarded the severity of his illness but actually sought out dangerous encounters. Accompanying the Marines and the Rough Riders, he made it a point to remain in view of sniper fire. His weakened health ultimately caused him to collapse and fall into delirium on July 7. He was evacuated aboard a transport ship where he received no medical attention. The surgeon in charge simply ordered him to quarantine himself.

Pulitzer fired Crane after the *World* had printed an unsigned article, attributed to him, accusing the Seventy-First New York Volunteers of panic during a skirmish. Crane had been wrongly blamed for this reportage but could do nothing at the time to fight the injustice. He was not jobless for long; Hearst hired him immediately. Before returning to the war zone, however, Crane went to the Adirondack Mountains to consult Dr. Edward Trudeau, the world-famous lung specialist. He was told that he was suffering from active tuberculosis. Rather than rest and care for himself, he was back in Florida by July and then on to Puerto Rico for the final phase of the war, arriving in Havana prior to the Spanish surrender in 1898.

He remained in Havana after the cessation of hostilities and rented a room in a small boarding house. He wrote sketches of life in Havana—"Stephen Crane's Views of Havana"—for the New York *Journal*, and love verses entitled, "Intrigue," dedicated to Lily Brandon Munroe. He was out of touch with both Cora and friends during his stay in the Cuban capital. Since no one heard from Crane, he was reported "missing." The reason for Crane's cutting himself off from the world remains a mystery.

Crane did cable Cora during the first week of October, however, informing her that he was alive, although he did not return to England. By December, 1898, Crane was coughing up blood, but he continued to nourish his dream of buying a little ranch in Texas where the sun shone ever so brightly and the air was clean and dry. But Cora was adamant about remaining in England. What could be more wonderful than living in a mansion in England and frequenting distinguished men of letters? In England, too, she finally seemed rid of her reputation as the proprietress of a brothel.

Cora finally won out and Crane agreed to return to England where he faced enormous debts. He arrived on January 11, 1899, a shadow of what he had been: thin, weak, and wracked by cough. His friends, such as Conrad and Wells, were relieved to know that he was alive.

No sooner had Crane set foot on English soil, however, than creditors started to hound him. He began writing nonstop. By February, his malarial fevers struck again. His illness, however, did not lessen the urgings of his creditors. And so, despite his weakened condition, Crane kept on writing stories, some of which were included in the Whilomville collection.

While Crane was in Cuba, Cora had found a magnificent estate dating back to the fourteenth century: Brede Place. She wrote him about it and he agreed to renting it. It would give Cora the stature she wanted and enhance Crane's social standing as well. But the upkeep of such an estate was far beyond their means. The impractical couple thought only of the pleasures such an ambience would give them. Unfortunately, the house was not only expensive but also damp, drafty, and cold, particularly in Crane's study, where he spent so much time. Conrad, James, Ford, and W. H. Hudson considered it a miracle Crane was able to do any writing at all.

Crane had yet another dream: to cover the Boer War as a correspondent. He did not, however, go to

South Africa, but instead accompanied his niece, Helen, to Lausanne and then went on to Paris to meet Cora. There he suffered another attack of malaria. Sequestering himself in his hotel room, he wrote some of *The Whilomville Stories* in order to pay for the hotel. After returning to England, he signed a contract for his Irish novel, *The O'Ruddy*. His Spanish-American War tales were soon to appear under the title *Wounds in the Rain* (1901), as were "Great Battles," sketches about well-known military encounters. Still, money was increasingly scarce and debts were mounting.

Three days after Christmas in 1899, Crane helped to write a play based on the legend of the Brede Manor, which was supposed to be haunted. *The Ghost*, a composite of comedy, farce, and burlesque, was written by ten friends including James, Conrad, Wells, Rider Haggard, Robert Barr, and A. E. Mason. Each of the characters was taken from the writings of one of the contributors: Doctor Moreau came from H. G. Wells's *Island of Doctor Moreau*; Peter Quint from James's *Turn of the Screw*; Rufus Coleman from *Active Service*, and so on. Performed before Sussex folk and Crane's thirty or forty invited guests, *The Ghost* was declared a great success. The following night, a banquet and ball were held at Brede Manor. The snowstorm that raged on the night of the ball added excitement to the merriment. But underneath the happiness and joy ran feelings of anguish. Even though nothing was said, the guests knew in their hearts that Crane was gravely ill and that he was doing his best to conceal it from Cora and his friends. At the end of the evening, however, Crane collapsed from a lung hemorrhage. Wells, having himself suffered from tuberculosis as a young man, understood the gravity of the situation and rode seven miles on a bicycle in the snow and ice to fetch a doctor.

After a few days, having recovered somewhat, Crane began writing again and going about his usual activities. On April 3, 1900, he suffered another hemorrhage. One of the doctors who was consulted said that there was little hope for Crane's recovery while others believed only one lung had been affected. Crane grew weaker each day. Some doctors now advised a sea voyage, but others thought he should go to a sanatorium. Crane was convinced he would get well. He began toying with the idea of going to St. Helena for the *New York Journal*, the *London Daily Chronicle* and the *Morning Post* to interview soldiers interned at the Boer prison camp.

Crane suffered another hemorrhage on April 30. His friends urged Cora to take him to Davos in the Swiss Alps or have him undergo the "Nordracht treatment" at a spa in Badenweiler in Germany's Black Forest. The second alternative was decided upon, a costly trip, since Crane had to go by stretcher and invalid carriage. Friends and admirers, including Andrew Carnegie, contributed to this futile undertaking, which was to be a *marche funèbre*.

Upon his arrival at the spa, noted for its restorative cures since the sixteenth century, Crane was carried to his second-floor apartment. Chills, fever, delirium set in, and under these conditions he relived the anguished moments described in "The Open Boat" when he was being tossed about amid the furious seas in the little dinghy. His life could not be saved now, and Stephen Crane died on June 5, 1900 at the age of twenty-eight.

Cora brought his body back to New York for burial. The funeral was held at the Metropolitan Temple on Seventh Avenue near Fourteenth Street, and the oration was delivered by the Reverend Dr. James M. Buckley. Few outside of family and friends were present. Crane was interred in the Evergreen Cemetery in Hillside, New Jersey. The granite tombstone simply reads:

Stephen Crane — Poet — Author — 1871–1900.

Part II

The Novels

By beauty of course I mean truth, for the one involves the other; it is only the false in art which is ugly, and it is only the false which is immoral. The truth may be indecent, but it cannot be vicious, it can never corrupt or deprave; and I should say this in defence of the grossest material honestly treated in modern novels as against the painted and perfumed meretriciousness of the novels that went before them. I conceive that apart from all the clamor about schools of fiction is the question of truth, how to get it in, so that it may get itself out again as beauty, the divinely living thing, which all men love and worship. So I make the truth the prime test of a novel. If I do not find that it is like life, then it does not exist for me as art; it is ugly, it is ludicrous, it is impossible.

—William Dean Howells,
"Novel-Writing and Novel
Reading: An Impersonal Explanation"

2

Maggie:
A Girl of the Streets

"It is inevitable that you will be greatly shocked by this book but continue please with all possible courage to the end," Crane wrote to his mentor, Hamlin Garland, about his first novel, *Maggie: A Girl of the Streets*. "For it tries to show that environment is a tremendous thing in the world and frequently shapes lives regardless. If one proves that theory, one makes room in heaven for all sorts of souls (notably an occasional street girl) who are not confidently expected to be there by many excellent people."[1] *Maggie* is not just a reportage of New York's Bowery slum and the saga of alienated beings; it is a work of art — in some ways akin to today's "multimedia" experience, a visual, audible, richly sensual tone poem.

The first draft of *Maggie* was written in 1891 when Crane was a student at Syracuse University. Having had virtually no firsthand experience with the "wicked city," Crane moved to New York City in the fall of 1892 to immerse himself in the environment he was describing. With two friends he shared a large room on the second floor of a boarding house on Avenue A (Eastern Boulevard then).[2]

As a space-paid reporter bursting with youthful vigor, he made the Bowery a kind of port of call. The late night hours usually were spent writing: he revised *Maggie* three times. Crane was poor, his clothes were threadbare, and he was shoeless in his rubber boots even during the harshest days of winter, but his spirits were not dampened. Instead, he felt a kinship to the bums and Bowery folk; he wanted to *know* them intimately, and his enthusiasm ran high. He was determined to become a great realist writer. Walking the streets with gusto, he learned, absorbed, and eagerly listened to the music of the people's language and the rhythms of their voices; he took in their gestures, gait, and stance and made of it all one sweeping synoptic image. He talked to all types: the Bowery boys, whose perfumed and slicked-down hair and skin-tight pants attracted the looks of many a passerby; prostitutes for whom he felt great compassion as well as an erotic attraction; derelicts who lived in tenements and frequented dives and saloons. In sum, Crane sought to know and understand all of seething humanity as it clustered so compactly in one single area in New York City.

Crane felt that to hobnob with this world would not only lend authenticity to his writing but would also help him to cut loose from his puritanical family and their values, which had weighed so heavily upon him. At last Crane was on his own; he breathed freely of the fullness of life in the forbidden but fascinating world that previously had spelled "sin" to him. *Maggie* is the fruit of his first genuine adventure into a strange life: his mixing with society's outcasts.

Maggie tells a simple story. The children of an alcoholic mother and a sullen, weak father, Maggie, "who blossomed in a mud puddle," her brother Jimmie, and a baby, who died in childhood, are products of a harsh tenement life. An employee in a collar and cuff factory, Maggie is much taken by her brother's friend, "swaggering" Pete, the bartender. She sees him as a kind of knight in shining armor who one day will sweep her out of her pauper existence, lift her into a world of romance, and, above all, protect her from the dangers that surround her. Her dream, however, comes to a sudden halt after she yields to Pete's advances. Cast out of the house by her drunken mother, rejected by Pete, streetwalking becomes her only means of survival. Degraded, humiliated, and lonely, she ends her life by jumping into "the waters lapping oilily against timbers."[3]

Although *Maggie's* plot is admittedly banal, its mood, pace, and dramatization of Bowery life in all of its sordid details and its characters' infinitely interesting cant make this novel memorable. Crane's skill in depicting his characters makes them speak to us today, perhaps even more directly than at the time the book was published. The novel portrays the harsh realities of immigrant life in that era with its sweatshops and primitive use of violence to solve daily problems.

Modern, too, is the technique of framed tableaux that Crane used in composing *Maggie*. At times, he sharply focuses on individuals in slowly-paced delineations; at others, he pans frenetically, telescoping large spaces and groups of persons, either in a colorful array or in interplays of light and darkness.

Publishers were unwilling to risk printing what they considered to be a fragmented and overly honest work. Even more dangerous from their point of view were the profanities in the text, which were shocking, even unpalatable. Equally intolerable to them was Crane's depiction of a man of the cloth as a hypocrite. What were the redeeming features of this "slum novel?"

Maggie was published in 1893 at the author's expense under the pseudonym of Johnston Smith. The publisher, which specialized in medical and religious tracts, charged Crane the staggering price of 869 dollars for eleven-hundred copies, although Crane himself did much of the typesetting. He sold the coal-mining stock inherited from his father and borrowed the rest of the money to pay the high publication costs. His problems, however, remained unsolved, even after *Maggie* came out. Booksellers (except for Brentano's) refused to carry the novel. Critics reacted negatively to Crane's forthrightness, considering some of the scenes too melodramatic and the language improper. Hamlin Garland and William Dean Howells, however, praised Crane's work for the very reasons the others condemned it.[4]

Despite the good offices of Crane's friends, *Maggie* was not only a financial but also a literary failure. Of the eleven-hundred copies printed, Crane gave away about a hundred and used the rest for kindling during the cold winter months. This failure along with extreme poverty stalked the twenty-two-year-old Crane. Americans were not yet prepared for recreations of life as it really is or for the realistic cant of slum dwellers with its use of slang and profanity. Also condemned was Crane's use of a repetitive and limited, vocabulary in dialogue, which pointed up the primitive inarticulateness of his characters.

Sentimental novels were flooding the market as reformers sought to elevate souls. Writers such as Susan Warner, Maria Cummins, and Emma D. E. N. Southworth offered their readers a sense of moral rectitude. In their work, the virtuous destitute had their chance and the meek would inherit the earth. Charles Loring Brace's *The Dangerous Classes of New York* and the Reverend Thomas de Witt Talmage's *Night Side of City Life* were moralistic writings dealing with fallen girls, sin, repentance, and redemption. Jacob Riis gained popularity with his sociological study, *How the Other Half Lives* (1890). Melodramatic works were also in vogue: *Orphan Nell, The Lost Heir*, and *The Fortune's of a Bowery Girl*, to mention but a few best-sellers. These novels featured slum heroines and heroes in all of their identities and roles; some protagonists became ballet dancers, artists, or happily married wives and mothers, lifted out of their wretched existences by good-doers. Why shouldn't readers prefer illusions to a painful and often repulsive reality?

American readers, for the most part, were accustomed to French romantic novels and plays, which often narrated the sagas of poor girls swept away by a prince charming, living happily ever after in luxury and love. Other works featured redeemed prostitutes whose purity of soul turned them into saints or poor children adopted by kindly people. Wasn't this the essence of Victor Hugo's novel, *Les Misérables*, and his play, *Marion Delorme*, which extolled the prostitute's capacity for self-sacrifice and beauty of soul? Alexandre Dumas's *The Lady of the Camellias* and Anatole France's *Thaïs* both underscored the courtesan's bent for self-abnegation.

Maggie, however, was an authentic recreation of slum life as Crane saw it. The reasons for his attraction to the seedy side of life and the world of the downtrodden are complex and perhaps will never be understood in a satisfactory manner. It is well to recall that Crane's parents were dedicated to healing souls, giving alms and sermonizing, but that Crane, in contrast, saw the conventional churchgoer as a smug, self-satisfied dispenser of charity. The dichotomy existing between his idealization of the heart's true goodness and the specious reality of brotherhood as practiced in the institutionalized church was immense. Other factors also may have contributed to Crane's fascination with the subculture of New York: a morbid form of masochistim, and a need to identify with the rejected.

Jimmie's Fight

The opening of *Maggie* creates the ambience and the emotional climate of the novel as it describes visceral street people who lead rough lives in a world where violence reigns, where might makes right.

A very little boy stood on a heap of gravel for the honour of Rum Alley. He was throwing stones at howling urchins from Devil's Row, who were circling madly about the heap and pelting him. His infantile countenance was livid with the fury of battle. His small body was writhing in the delivery of oaths.

Struggle and danger predominate here as they do throughout the novel. Two factions, two points of view, are fighting it out, each attempting to crush the underdog. Although the rival gangs—Rum Alley and Devil's Row—are mentioned by name, they are also metaphors for a larger antagonism: the conflict between good and evil that exists within each individual as well as within society and the universe.

That *Maggie* is not merely an account of slum life, but also is meant to represent eternal symbols, is attested to by the fact that in the first draft of his novel Crane did not give his characters proper names. They were identified by epithets: Maggie, for example, was the girl who "blossomed in a mud-puddle"; Pete, her seducer, was a "knight"; Nell, her rival, was the "woman of brilliance and audacity." Only after his friends had convinced him to do so, did Crane give names to the creatures of his imagination. Had they remained anonymous—as is so frequently the case in contemporary novels—the mythical quality of the work would have been that much more pronounced.

Jimmie and the other urchins in Crane's opening passage have been raised in violence, which assures their survival. The "very little boy," Jimmie, knows this. Determined to vanquish his enemies who circle beneath him, this "little champion of Rum Alley" with his tattered clothes and bloodied, cut, and bruised face represents the life-force that struggles to preserve whatever it considers its own, here a living space. When Jimmie does run down the side of the heap of gravel, avoiding the stones hurled at him, he obeys his instincts, but a stone hurled by one of the rival gang "smashes in Jimmie's mouth." Blood gushes. Tears splatter. Pain and anger cohabit in that small, spindly frame. Jimmie reels, but he keeps on his course amid the screaming and jeering of his enemies.

A "boastfully sauntering lad" of sixteen enters the picture. A sharpy with his hat tipped over one eye and a cigar stump "tilted at the angle of defiance in his mouth," he already is wearing "the chronic sneer of an ideal manhood" on his lips. There is no doubt that Pete will challenge anyone who thwarts him: "he held victory in his fists." The epithets used to depict this youth are indicative of his approach to life: aggressive, arrogant, power-conscious. This "swaggering" lad encourages Jimmie to pursue alone his fight against the enemy. And so the battle rages on in "a bobbing circle" around him.

To underscore the eternal quality of warring principles in humankind — whether among slum folk or other social classes — Crane uses the symbol of the circle. The fighting urchins "circling madly about," the "cursing circle," and the "circle of little boys" emphasize the perpetual nature of all conflict.

Quickly, Crane focuses on a different scene: an older man carrying a "dinner-pail" and smoking an applewood pipe. He plods along the avenue, his eyes "sullen" and "listless." As he looks at the fighters, he suddenly recognizes his son, Jimmie, on the ground fighting with another boy. He kicks into "the chaotic mass on the ground," and the boys disentangle themselves. Jimmie "totters away," humiliation added to the physical injuries he has suffered. "The little champion" has not only lost his battle but is hauled away by his father. How can he ever save face?

By setting the scene outdoors, Crane makes the world of the child plain for all to see. Impulses and

instincts are given free reign. Darker elements will intrude, however, in the next episode when shadowy and
murky pulsations emerge in all of their insidious viru-
lence.

The Mother

The second image, which is that of the adult world, is a
replica of the first, but more subtly rendered. Slum
life is played out in the tenebrous apartment houses
with their networks of "gruesome doorways," slovenly
dressed women carrying babies, and clothes fluttering
out of windows in an early autumn wind. Foul smells
emanate from these dank, miasmic tenements: the
odors of poverty.

Maggie, a "small ragged girl," walks along the
somber street, dragging along impatiently her baby
brother, Tommie, a "red, bawling infant." Across the
street, she sees her father and Jimmie approaching.
She scolds the lad for having fought yet another battle.
Unabashed, although he lost the fight, Jimmie lets his
pride take over. He resents his sister's rebukes because
he looks upon himself as a hero, proud of sporting a
bloodstained face and multiple bruises. He shows his
anger in the only way he knows how — by slapping her.

The four enter one of those "dark stairways" and
long "cold, gloomy halls." The iciness and prisonlike
atmosphere of the apartment building is a metaphor for
the lack of communication and understanding within
families in general and the Johnson family in particular. Between the parents and children, there is no rapport, no solicitude, no warmth, and no real love.

Only after the father pushes open the door to the
apartment is the reader struck by the horror of the
mother, Marie Johnson. The massive shoulders of this
large woman "dominated the dirt, the disorder of this

dimly lit room. "Eh what? Been fightin' again!" she shrieked, giving vent to her anger, grasping the urchin, shaking him, dragging him to the sink and scrubbing his lacerated face. Jimmie struggles valiantly to dislodge himself from his mother's vise-like grip, but fails in the attempt.

A formidable mother and a weak-willed father dominate life within the apartment, as Pete controlled the situation in the fighting scene. The terrifying mother figure with her gigantic power and enormous body — "massive shoulders," "huge arms," "immense hands," a "chieftain-like stride" — is archetypal in dimension. She is a destructive earth mother who crushes her offspring, a female Cronus who ingests her brood. Holding weakness in contempt, she scorns her husband and the younger members of the family. That the "babe crawled under the table" to get out of her way indicates the feelings of those who live under the roof of this animal-like creature.

The mother is a paradigm of failure on all levels. Unable to control mangled emotions or face her own emptiness and the absurdity of her condition, she takes to drinking. When the sullen-eyed father gathers up courage now and then to reprimand her for yielding to drink, she unleashes a series of invectives, repudiating his accusations.

Crane uses language as a dramatic vehicle to describe life in the Johnson family. Sounds becomes a tool to coerce the readers into identifying with one of the protagonists or into rejecting them all. Screams and howls reverberate through the apartment along with the clatter of dishes and the hissing noises of cooking potatoes. Crooning, strident, and concrete sounds intrude from outside into this darkened lair, increasing the tempo and excitement of the already volatile atmosphere. "Eh, child, what is it dis time? Is yer fader beatin' yer mudder, or yer mudder beatin' ye fader?" question the neighbors.

Above the muffled road of conversation, the dismal wailing of babies at night, the thumping of feet in unseen corridors and rooms, and the sound of varied hoarse shoutings in the street and the rattling of wheels over cobbles, they heard the screams of the child and the roars of the mother die away to a feeble moaning and subdued bass muttering.

Jimmie, Maggie, and Pete

Time elapses during which the babe and father die. Jimmie is now a young man with his soul clad in "armour." He has no illusions. Fighting was and still is his language. Abstract principles of love, peace, charity, and redemption as preached by men of the cloth are of no interest either to Jimmie or to the hungry who believe that soup-tickets lead more speedily to salvation than the fanciest homilies. Church and money are the same to most of Crane's characters. "Above all things he despised obvious Christians and ciphers with the chrysanthemums of aristocracy in their buttonholes. He considered himself above both of these classes. He was afraid of nothing."

Jimmie is a truck-driver, who allows no one to stand in the way of his pair of "champing horses" as they plough through one of New York's most crowded streets crammed full of drays and carts and people. Jimmie seems to be leading a charmed life, master of his destiny as he dominates events.

Like his father, Jimmie smokes a pipe as he sits at home in the evening, serene in his temporary withdrawal from the chaotic world. Bluster and muscle dictate his acts, but there is nevertheless something poetic about him. On certain evenings, Crane wrote, he looks at the moon with reverence, relating to this universal force of nature. On other occasions, he seems almost tender and kind to his sister, Maggie.

Maggie "blossomed in a mud-puddle." Although never really described by Crane, the reader has the feeling that she is very beautiful. To be noted is her passivity throughout the novel. Coerced by family and friends and forced into situations rather than determining them, she is the opposite of her mother who, brimming with power, has deprived her daughter of all of her vitality. But Maggie is not lazy; she works long hours making collars and cuffs in a sweatshop of a shirt factory. Only after she meets Pete, the "swaggering lad" who had prodded Jimmie to pursue the fight in the opening scene, does she long for some other kind of existence.

One evening, Pete, now a bartender, invites Jimmie to a boxing bout and calls for him at the Johnson apartment. Maggie is taken by his "nonchalance," his slick, debonair manner, his hair "curled down over his forehead in an oiled bang," his "pugged nose," his "bristling moustache of short, wire-like hairs"—all important details in Crane's portrait of a man destined to play an important role in Maggie's life. Pete is different from the other men she has met; he is elegantly dressed, in his "double-breasted coat, edged with black braid," a "red puff tie" and patent leather shoes. And "his mannerism stamped him as a man who had a correct sense of his personal superiority." Appearance is all that is important to Pete.

Maggie looks admiringly at Pete and unconsciously begins to retreat into the shadowy parts of the living room—into the "mud-puddle," her natural habitat. His "half-closed eyes" fascinate her as does the way he tells stories. "Here was a formidable man who disdained the strength of a world full of fists. Here was one who had contempt for brash-clothed power; one whose knuckles could ring defiantly against the granite of law. He was a knight." Pete's sudden appearance on the scene is like an epiphany, filling Maggie with wistful awe. How could he, an "aristocrat," enter the Johnson's apartment with its broken furniture, its grimy walls, its dirt and disorder? He becomes her "ideal man" a prince charming who could sweep her out of her squalor. Like Flaubert's Emma Bovary, who also lived out her romantic ideas, Maggie identifies Pete with "far-away lands where the little hills sing together in the morning." She daydreams, visualizing herself in paradisiacal gardens, walking along in her lover's embrace.

Crane remains objective, but there is an undertone of ironic deprecation, ever so subtle, of the naive, good-natured Maggie who is utterly ignorant of the world. By diminishing the size of objects within the Johnson living room and thus altering its proportions, Crane implies a similar diminution of Maggie's own wavering self-confidence and increased sense of inadequacy. She feels "unfit to hold his [Pete's] dignity, the attribute of a supreme warrior."

Pete eventually becomes interested in Maggie. "Say, Mag, I'm stuck on yer shape. It's outa sight," he says grinning, eying her up and down. After leaving the Johnson apartment, Maggie peers out of the window, following his image now enclosed in a halo of glory.

Maggie is much too naive and perhaps too unintelligent ever to understand and properly judge people or situations. Hungry for affection and love, she muses about how to impress this "knight" of hers. Finally she thinks of a way. Having saved part of her week's pay, she will purchase flowered cretonne to make him a lambrequin. When he visits the following Sunday, he will be pleased to see it hanging on "the slightly careening mantel over the stove in the kitchen." But he does not show up that day, and Maggie feels ashamed of her efforts. He, the "knight" errant, is above such things. She then imagines the many girls he must have at his beck and call and draws fanciful sketches of the incredible Pete, dressed in new clothes as he takes her to all sorts of places. Then, looking at herself in comparison, she sees only a "mouse-coloured" person, ineffectual and commonplace. As Maggie's real-life situation deteriorates, her dream world takes on greater amplitude.

Returning home one night, Maggie finds her mother drunk, "with lurid face and tossing hair," cursing and destroying the furniture in the room." She then falls into a stupor amid the "wreck of chairs," the "fragments of various household utensils" scattered about. In her besotted fury, she has torn Maggie's lambrequin to shreds: "it lay in a bedraggled heap in the corner," in the shadows—a premonitory image of Maggie's fate.

Sanctuaries

Sanctuaries are enclosed, protected areas into which people withdraw to find safety and comfort, or to be healed. Maggie enters these limited zones—the beer hall, the theatre, a variety of saloons—to live out her dreams. Ultimately deemed impure, unworthy, and offensive, she is cast out of these symbolically holy places to her doom.

Maggie is thrilled when Pete brings her to the working man's beer hall, a nice, family-oriented place with dancing and lively entertainment:

An orchestra of yellow silk women and bald-headed men, on an elevated stage near the centre of a great green-hued hall, played a popular waltz. The place was crowded with people grouped about little tables. A batallion of waiters slid among the throng, carrying trays of beer-glasses, and making change from the inexhaustible vaults of their trousers pockets. Little boys, in the costumes of French chefs, paraded up and down the irregular aisles vending fancy cakes.

And Pete knows just how to place orders for beer, impressing Maggie still further with his savoir faire. "Gracious and attentive, "considering her above all else, he was — of this she was certain — a highly "cultured gentle-men" since he talked so condescendingly to the waiters.

Maggie is mesmerized by what she sees: a dancer who "galloped upon the stage," her pink and lacy skirts flying high as she kicks and frolics about in rhythmic interludes; a ventriloquist holding "two fantastic dolls on his knees"; a singer "of debatable age," whose reper-toire ranges from black spirituals to Irish ditties, con-cluding with "The Star-Spangled Banner." When Mag-gie enters into the spirit of things along with the others, she is transported, momentarily at least, from a drab existence into a land of fancy.

When Pete takes Maggie home that night, he asks, "Say, Mag, give us a kiss for takin' yet t' d' show, will yer?" She laughs. "Naw, Pete, dat wasn't in it", she answers, withdrawing into her house and then running up the stairs to the relative safety of her apartment.

Maggie's introduction to night life and all its ex-citement increases her dissatisfaction with the collar and cuff establishment where she is obliged to spend so many hours each day. The noises of the sewing ma-chines and the passing elevated trains deafen her, and she is repulsed by the odors of garbage heaped inside and outside of the building. A sense of decay and of uselessness fill her world. She longs to be like other women, to buy new dresses, to have soft white hands. Now that she is in love with Pete, she feels her isolation from the other women at work even more keenly and realizes that she has no friends.

Pete invites her to other sanctuaries; more and more he "loomed like a golden sun" in her life. In the dime museum, she views deformed beings of all types. Another fascinating world is found in the Central Park Menagerie, and still a different one — higher perhaps — in the Museum of Art. And Maggie "giggled with glee." At the theatre, she loves to see the many romantic heroines peopling the stage — those poor, sad beings living in such tawdry surroundings but always rescued by some great person and then placed in gorgeous palaces or elegant estates. Villiany is forever annihilated. Maggie identifies with the events on stage, losing "herself in sympathy with the wanderers swooning in snow-storms beneath happy-hued church windows, while a choir within sang 'Joy to the World.'" She joins the audiences as they react to stage events: "The loud gallery was overwhelmingly with the unfortunate and the oppressed. . . . When anybody died in the pale-green snow-storms, the gallery mourned." For Maggie, observing events is experiencing "transcendental realism." This is life. Maggie sees herself as a heroine of this melodrama.

> She rejoiced at the way in which the poor and virtuous eventually overcame the wealthy and wicked. The theatre made her think. She wondered if the culture and refinement she had seen imitated, perhaps grotesquely, by the heroine on the stage, could be acquired by a girl who lived in a tenement house and worked in a shirt factory.

Like Emma Bovary, Maggie's innocence does not elicit the author's pity or compassion, but merely scorn. "The root of Bowery life," Crane wrote, "is a sort of cowardice."[5] Many succeed in rising above adverse circumstances; others wither in the morass of passivity.

The saloon, looked upon as a sanctuary where the magic of drink can bring forgetfulness, also has its rules and regulations. Maggie's mother, for example, has been forcibly ejected from its portals; passersby laugh and jeer as they watch her lurch "heavily out on the sidewalk."

As Maggie's mother makes her way up the stairs to the apartment, anger marks her face — she seems ready for a fight. When Jimmie sees her and tries to force her into the apartment, she raises her arm "and whirled her great fist at her son's face." Although he evades this thrust, the struggle between mother and son begins. Maggie watches the painful scene and then passively retreats into the darkness of the other room. The storm has almost wrecked the apartment; furniture and crockery are broken, the stove is out of place, pipes are burst, and water is flowing everywhere. When Pete takes Maggie away from this brawling existence, the mother assails them.

Days pass. Neighbors whisper that they've heard Maggie "was a-crying as if her heart would break, poor t'ing." Jimmie listens to this gossip in a fury. Now he sees himself playing the role of his sister's comforter and protector and, to defend her, he is even ready to kill Maggie's lover. With this thought in mind, he goes looking for Pete in the bartender's home territory: "a glass-fronted building shed" which casts "a yellow glare upon the pavement." The color yellow gives the reader a clue to the events to follow. Yellow for Crane personifies evil, degradation, and death.

"The open mouth of a saloon called seductively to passengers to enter and annihilate sorrow or create rage," Crane writes about Pete's territory. Like an animal's open gullet, it swallows those who enter its precincts. No one escapes the jaws, the gnashing teeth, the wild, savage sneer of the saloon. Its mirrors, set about the sideboard, seem to enlarge its size while lending it a still more dazzling aura. Mirrors, lights, glasses, a nickel-plated cash register—all glitter under the glare of the gas lamps. Pete, in his "white jacket," is the majestic bartender as he deals out his foam-topped drinks, each of which is a kind of rite of passage to a world of whimsy and joy. Jimmy enters with a friend. They both order a gin and then begin riling Pete, who turns on them: "Drink yer stuff an' git out an' don' make no trouble." Pete shoots "a lurid glance at Jimmie." Jimmie, "the little champion," as he was called earlier, starts "to swell with valour."

A fight among the three breaks out—a variation on the opening scene. But now, in the world of the adults, Crane describes each of the punches as if he were a Thomas Eakins detailing one of the legendary bouts of John Sullivan—that bare-knuckle boxer, America's first great sports hero. Crane's camera lens captures vicious sweeps of arms and legs and the fighters' broad shoulders and fire-flinging eyes. This is no ordinary fight; these are no ordinary beings. Like Promethean figures, they have become cosmic forces, aspects of eternal combatants. The vigor of Crane's incredible prose and the flow of its rhythms are worthy of Céline at his best. The three brawlers spark the entire saloon into joining the battle, and tumult spreads. Plates and bottles are hurled as missiles, shattering what had been so tidy and controlled. Pete's world, like the mirrors all around, "splintered to nothing."

Although he has fought with Jimmie, Pete continues his affair with Maggie, but on a different level. Instead of the theatre and family-oriented beer halls, they now frequent a lower-class dive, where frowsy-haired women in soiled evening dresses sit with men who eye the scantily attired entertainers. Maggie by now has lost whatever assurance and self-esteem she may have once had. Increasingly timid about Pete, who is drifting away from her, she nevertheless still dares to hope for his tenderness. Her misery only increases his power over her. He struts about the saloon: a "lion of lordly characteristics." He enjoys ordering people about—waiters for the most part—leaning back on his chair and looking at them with undisguised contempt. Still, Maggie feels some comfort when she goes out with him, and he is still proud of her: "Mag, yer a bloomin' good looker."

Three weeks have passed since Maggie left home. Sitting calmly with Pete by her side, she watches the beer glasses being emptied amid the chatter and clatter of buzzing humanity. Suddenly, a voice calls out to

Pete, tearing Maggie from her dream world. She sees his "eyes sparkle" as he gazes upon the handsome woman. They talk for a while and then walk out together. Maggie feels like a wounded animal.

The Suicide

There are no more sanctuaries for Maggie. She returns home to her mother who castigates her daughter for having sullied the Johnson name. Her bellowing voice attracts the neighbors, who stand around listening to rage and scorn being piled upon Maggie. Jimmie sympathizes with his sister at first, but then sides with his mother.

Unable to bear the pain of rejection and having lost what she thought to be Pete's love, Maggie leaves and makes her way to Pete's bar, hoping he will take her back. But Pete is now ashamed of her. She will sully the reputation of the bar where he works. Her presence makes him uncomfortable, and wanting to get rid of her, he tells her so. When she asks where she should go, Pete grows exasperated: "Oh, go to hell!" he yells, slamming the door in her face. But eventually Pete also will be degraded when he's knocked unconscious in another fight and then robbed by streetwalkers.

Passive, cipherlike, faceless, Maggie wanders away into the night. Men look at her, wanting her, but she hurries along, passing rows of houses and dark, dismal alleyways. Encountering "a stout gentleman in a silk hat and a chaste black coat, whose decorous row of buttons reached from his chin to his knees," she realizes he is a man of God. Surely he will help her if she approaches him. "His beaming chubby face was a picture of benevolence and kind-heartedness. His eyes shone good will". But as she approaches him, he withdraws in shock. He will not go near her, not even "to save a soul."

Months pass. Maggie now knows the world of the prostitute, which leaves her still more lonely. No longer able to bear the horror of it all, she walks into the shadows of the night and then jumps in the river to her death.

The Farce

The Mother is eating when Jimmie tells her Maggie is dead. At first, she will not believe it and continues her meal. Then she weeps, reminiscing about her daughter when she was a child. "I kin remember her when her two feet was no bigger dan yet t'umb, and she weared worsted boots," she laments, with an air of self-indulgence, basking in her righteousness, certain of her own stolid virtues.

When the neighbors gather in the hall, her moans grow louder. She did so much for her daughter, she says, and the neighbors agree, sobbing along with her. The girl was simply misguided. Let her end be a lesson for others who disobey the commandments of virtue. "Yeh'll fergive her, Mary! Yeh'll fergive yer bad bad chil'," says a neighbor to the mother, echoing similar sentiments. "She's gone where her sins will be judged," the others lament in turn. "Deh Lord gives and deh Lord takes away," another woman echos in response. The sun beams through the window during this interlude, "lending a ghastly cheerfulness upon the faded hues of the room." As for the Mother, she answers the questions of neighbors amid tears and screams of pain, "Oh, yes, I'll fergive her! I'll fergive her!" she says with all the self-righteousness of a woman blinded by her own beclouded vision.

Crane's farce-like depiction of this last scene is unforgettable: the self-indulgent mother forgiving the daughter she had thrown out of her house, the very person for whom she felt no compassion and whose

very existence she never even acknowledged. The sham
of her lamentations is a stinging mockery of the very
notion of love and charity fostered by the mission
churches, which Crane constantly and harshly de-
rided.[6]

Bitter irony and anger dominate in *Maggie* as each
scene is etched out in jarring language. Morality is
presented as destructive, sentiment as treacherous,
men of the cloth as hypocritical, and the family as
breeding only wretchedness.

Crane disdained sham romanticism. He believed,
as did Garland and Howells, that in order to be art
writing must be based on reality, be it sordid or brutal.
"I cannot see why people hate ugliness in art. Ugliness
is just a matter of treatment."[7] True art, Crane now
understood, is the "child of suffering."

Most reviews were unfavorable when *Maggie* was
first published, but when the novel was printed com-
mercially three years later by Appleton in New York
and Heinemann in England, the critical reception was
uniformly positive: "the strongest piece of slum writing," a "powerful sermon," "one of the most downright
earnestly-written books ever published."[8] Times and
tastes had changed.

3

The Red Badge of Courage

The Red Badge of Courage was "born of pain — despair,"
Crane wrote.[1] He was referring to not only the pain
and despair of the foot soldier fighting in the Civil
War — the major theme of the novel — but the terror and
excoriating hurt that come with the living out of a rite
of passage, here the transition from adolescence to
manhood. Written thirty years after the end of the war
between the North and South, the episodes in *The Red
Badge of Courage* are fictionalized reality that may also be
viewed as testing stages in the psychological evolution
of Crane's protagonist, Henry Fleming.

Two years had passed since the publication of *Maggie*
during which Crane had begun another novel, *George's
Mother* (1896) and a collection of poetry, *Black Riders*
(1895), deeply felt verses of rare beauty. He found it
easier, he said, to convey his thoughts and feelings in
poetry rather than in prose. Lines and stanzas seemed
to gush from him spontaneously and without effort.
But Crane's poems met with one rejection after another. Publishers found his verses not only unconventional
but also iconoclastic and predicted they would only
alienate readers. Still Crane persevered writing poetry
while working on *The Red Badge of Courage*.

Living in the old Art Students League building
with three artist friends, he usually wrote at night and
then slept most of the day. Upon completion of the

novel, after some seven drafts, Crane took the manuscript to a publisher, S. S. McLure who kept it for six
months without giving the author an answer. When,
after six months he received no answer, he took it to the
Irving Bacheller and Johnson syndicate, and sold
eighteen-thousand words of it to them for 90 dollars. It
first appeared in Philadelphia's and New York's *Press*;
D. Appleton and Company brought it out in book form
in October 1895.

Prior to its publication, Crane wanted to live out
one more dream. He had heard and read about the
fascinating macho cowboys of the West and was familiar with the *Police Gazette*, which reported the deeds of
these dissolute and lawless men. The fantastic tales of
gold miners who overnight made and lost fortunes also
had aroused his imagination. Crane, ever the boy at
heart, longed to talk with *real* Indians, see the wide
open spaces, deserts, badlands, and wilderness, and
experience for himself the romance attached to these
fabulous places. As thousands of young people before
him, he heeded the advice of the founder and editor of
the *New York Tribune*, Horace Greeley, who had said,
"Go West, young man, go West."

Crane set out for St. Louis on January 30, 1895 as
a roving reporter for the Bacheller syndicate. In Lincoln, he met the young Willa Cather, a junior at Nebraska State University, who worked in her spare time
at the offices of the Lincoln *State Journal*. Crane was "the
first man of letters I had ever met in the flesh," she
wrote years later.[2] With Cather, Crane felt at ease and
discussed his dreams, his future as a writer, and his
techniques: "The detail of a thing has to filter through
my blood, and then it comes out like a native product,
but it takes forever".[3] In the articles he sent home ("Ne-
braskans' Bitter Fight for Life" and others), Crane sided
politically and economically with the farmers whose
lives were dependent upon the vagaries of nature. Lou-

isiana, Arkansas, Arizona, Nevada, Colorado, Texas, and Mexico were all to feed his fertile imagination. In Mexico, he was introduced to a whole new culture, which he transmitted to his readers in such reports as "Mexican Sights and Street Scenes." His dispatches to Bacheller during this period appeared both as feature articles and news items in various newspapers throughout the country. He had plunged deeply into another exciting world. Masterpieces such as "The Bride Comes to Yellow Sky" (1897) and "The Blue Hotel" (1897) would be forthcoming. By October, 1895, laudatory reviews for *The Red Badge of Courage* were appearing, and Crane greeted them with elation.

The Red Badge of Courage was innovative stylistically as well as psychologically. Since the only experience Crane had had with war was military maneuvers at prep school, he had to supplement his scant knowledge of the Civil War with considerable research on the event. Crane studied such works as *Battles and Leaders of the Civil War*, a four volume account written mostly by veterans of the war; Warren Lee Goss's *Recollections of a Private*, depicting the feelings of enlisted men during battle and the panic encountered at Bull Run; and the *Personal Memoirs of Ulysses S. Grant*, which gave an authentic political and social picture of the causes leading to the Civil War. He also perused Mathew Brady's extraordinary photographs, which were taken in the midst of the fighting.

Crane, however, was not interested in military strategy and tactics. What makes *The Red Badge of Courage* extraordinary is the vivid descriptions and beautifully cadenced prose, some of which is sheer poetry. Its varied rhythms frequently parallel the emotions of the characters, allowing Crane to inject suspense into the situations he describes. His use of alliteration, assonance, and onomatopeia heightens the nerve-searing impact of military retreats and the push of advancing columns. The auditory effects of his prose range from harsh, grating, strident and ear-piercing cacophonies to mellifluous and subdued harmonies. The sounds of words play their part in beating out the rhythm of the life and death ordeal of the military man.

Mention must also be made of the powerful visual aspect of Crane's writing. Panoramic descriptions of battle scenes are etched out in detail: whole armies waiting in the mud or on the grass, forced to think about their fate, sweating it out until their unit is called upon to go into battle; wounded agonizing men, clashing muskets, cocked rifles, and shellfire crackling here and there as luminosities flare in the distance. The reader is not in the presence of the impressionism of a Monet or a Renoir with daubs of colors pressed onto the canvas here and there in an array of gentle and beauteous hues. Crane's world is cruel, violent, and visceral, reminiscent of the huge war canvases of Gros, Géricault, and Delacroix. Also Winslow Homer's influence is discernible in some of Crane's powerfully textured scenes. Likewise, Ole Peter Hansen Balling's canvas of "Grant and his Generals" may have influenced certain vividly rendered scenes in *The Red Badge of Courage*: the complacency of some of the men as contrasted with the frenzy of others as they march into battle; the searing sun burning down on the soldiers as the flag flies high in the background; the sharply outlined forms of sweating and bloodied horses thrashing about or galloping across battlefields.

To increase the collective appeal of events — perhaps singling out the Battle of Chancellorsville to focus upon — Crane used the narrative voice of an observer whose talk beats into the reader's mind, making the reader a passionate participant. By not using names for the most part, but substituting epithets in their stead, Crane injected an allegorical quality into his work. "It was essential that I should make my battle a type and name no names,"[4] he stated; and so, his characters may be regarded as parts of a whole, each pointing up a specific characteristic of man, both in Crane's time and in ours.

The Red Badge of Courage narrates the ordeal of an illusion-filled youth who dreams of being a hero but, faced with the actual terror of battle, runs from the scene. The allegorical figures he meets in the course of the action and his feelings of shame and guilt both serve to increase his consciousness of himself as an individual and of the bond that ties him to his fellow soldiers. The rite of passage from dreamy-eyed youth to manhood may be analyzed in several stages: the separation, the dark night of the soul, the initiation into the patriarchal fold, the forest experience, the reintegration, and the rebirth.

The Separation

The panoramic opening image of *The Red Badge of Courage* sets the stage and tone of the work. Nature, although outwardly at peace, emits rumblings of disquietude from the deep. The reader first sees, as in Genesis, a vast, unified world that then separates into heaven and earth, light and darkness, engendering conflict in the divisive process:

The cold passed reluctantly from the earth, and the retiring fogs revealed an army stretched out on the hills, resting. As the landscape changed from brown to green, the army awakened, and began to tremble with eagerness at the noise of rumors. It cast its eyes upon the roads, which were growing from long troughs of liquid mud to proper thoroughfares. A river, amber-tinted in the shadow of its banks, purled at the army's feet; and at night, when the stream had become of a sorrowful blackness, one could see across it the red, eyelike gleam of hostile camp-fires set in the low brows of distant hills.

The biblical cadence of the above passage came naturally to Crane, who was stepped in its writings from an early age. He responded powerfully to the poetics of the Bible, however much he rejected organized religion. This awesome image of expansive nature becomes archetypal as human individuality and subjectivity are transformed into universality and objectivity. The "cold" in the opening sentence conveys feelings of extreme solitude and isolation, reflecting the physical and psychological agony of the soldier waiting to be called into combat. Stasis congeals his emotions: he is fearful of what is ahead. In the personification of the "retiring fogs," there is also the sense that the veils hiding the unknown are lifting. The difficulties hidden from view, beyond one's tangled emotions, will emerge full force from their secret world. Colors, ranging from somnolent autumnal tones to fertile greens, convey the excited feelings of a personality waking to the life experience. The blackness of shadows are contrasted with a fiery, passionate, and seering red. Terror, shock, and the horror of death are lurking everywhere.

A "tall soldier," Jim Conklin, comes into view. He stands out above the crowd, not only because of his height but also because of his philosophy. He is returning from the brook, waving his shirt "bannerlike," a harbinger of important news: the soldiers are to go into battle the next day. No longer will they have to bear the intolerable tension of waiting. The tall soldier, as the leader he would like to be, then commands attention to listen to what proves to be a "tall" tale.

The "bannerlike" garment he waves in the wind may be regarded as the first emblem of the flag image that plays such a significant role in Crane's novel. Symbolizing the ideals of the army of the North, it represents a link between individual experience and the destiny of a nation to be unified. Its standard-bearer, the tall soldier, fills with hope the hearts of the restless men.

But the "youthful private," Henry Fleming, is a naive hometown boy, and when he discovers that the regiment is not about to move, he reacts harshly to this first encounter with false information. Withdrawing into himself, he goes into "his hut . . . crawl[ing] through an intricate hole that served as a door." Removing himself from the crowd gives him time to assess his feelings. The image of crawling used here by Crane is particularly apt. Like an infant or an animal, the youth seems to be getting down to the ground in his search for an answer, he withdraws into his own darkness in order to experience his yet untried potential. Once inside the hut, he lies down on his bunk to meditate and experience what St. John of the Cross referred to as "the dark night of the soul."

The Dark Night of the Soul

Every stage of development, be it the birth process or the step-by-step evolution of an artist, requires a wrench from a previous condition. Such a twist, sometimes violent, often entails discomfort and pain but also the anticipation of future joy. Just as the writer constructs what was "born of pain — despair," in Crane's words, so the youthful private builds his personality. In so doing, he must strengthen his nascent ego, the center of consciousness, which is initially weakly structured and fragmented.

In the makeshift hut, the youth's thoughts veer in various directions, introducing the reader to one of the most spectacular scenes in the novel. The dark side of the unconscious will be brought to light: inner dangers and uncertainties, which at the outset he experiences as pulsations, are articulated. Fantasies burgeon as irrational impulses contaminate his consciousness—dreams and hallucinations, demons and monsters, emerge. The callow youth sifts through the tangled feelings that plague him and, in the process, learns to discriminate and, above all, to *question* himself and others. No longer an easy target for those devastating forces that could destroy him, he learns to understand and confront those heaving impulses that besiege him.

In the blackness of the hut, the neophyte learns to think and to disentangle his muddled emotions. To clarify this process for the reader, Crane again uses his painter's palette: rays of light penetrate a small window, casting yellowish and golden hues into the formerly black room. Blackness no longer reigns supreme; forms and shadows become discernible as they take on contour. "Cracker boxes," used as furniture, come into view. Symbolically, they represent the lad's psychological situation. He is like the box that both incarcerates and protects the nourishment (or crackers) inside. Unless he releases his viselike hold on his unconscious, the riches contained within will remain imprisoned. Opened boxes may, like Pandora's, unleash miseries— but they may also bring hope.

Light shines into the youth's inner sanctum from another source: a "flimsy chimney." Here too, the ambivalent nature of the illuminating process is obvious. Fire could set the entire hut ablaze just as war can burn and destroy a soldier—or transform him into a hero. Psychological conflict may make one aware of one's own inner flame and one's libido, thereby expanding consciousness, but it may also lead to increased chaos and insanity.

The youthful private is described as entering into a "trance of astonishment"—a state resembling sleep where the unconscious takes over. He is stupefied, dazed, stunned, and inarticulate. At a loss for words, he fantasizes and so experiences an alteration of mood. No longer isolated from the rest of the men, he begins to identify with them. He sees himself as a hero, becoming part of "one of those great affairs of the earth."

During this period of introspection, he regresses into his past, a literary device used to acquaint readers with the lad's background. We learn that he was born and bred on a farm and that his mother "discouraged" him from enlisting in what he considered to be the Great Civil War. She looks with "contempt" upon "war ardor and patriotism" and feels it is more important for him to remain on the farm than go into the battlefield. Unaware of what it would be like to be separated from his environment and thrust into the military, the dreamy-eyed youth entertains thoughts of glory and the romance of battle. The very image of army life fills him with a "shiver in a prolonged ecstasy of excitement." When he enlists he finds the "beautiful scene" of parturition with his mother, which he "privately primed himself for," not at all what he imagined: "The Lord's will be done," she says as she continues milking the cow. There are no melodramatic goodbyes, but he does see two tears on his mother's face.

To reject the wishes of a parent represents the youth's first overt act of liberation. Siegfried, Roland, Achilles, and Parzival are among Henry Fleming's many other literary antecedents. At first the lad is dazzled by the ease of separation from what we may call the matriarchal world. He sees a clear way ahead for him with no impediments standing in the way of achieving his goal.

Even after the youth leaves for Washington, D.C. and begins musing on the essential meaning of war, he still views it as nothing but a series of "death struggles with small time in between for sleep and meals." He ponders the significance of the word death as his secular and religious education has offered him only abstract answers.

Another "great" thought preoccupies him in the hut. How will he react to battle? Although he feels attuned to the men in his regiment, a strange feeling gnaws at him. "He tried to mathematically prove to himself that he would not run from battle." Logic has to dominate at this juncture, rational and reductive reasoning are called upon to understand the irrational. Until now he admits, "he knew nothing of himself." How will he feel if he runs in the face of danger? Certainly, such cowardice would be shameful.

The "tall soldier" and the "loud soldier," Wilson, slide through the hole and join the youth in the hut. Still pondering his torturing question, Henry Fleming asks the tall soldier how he would perform in battle? Would he run away? He has thought of such a possibility, the tall soldier answers, then telling him that if others run, he would also "run like the devil", but if nobody ran, he would fight with his group. The tall soldier feels no shame at the thought of cowardice. He relates to the men of his regiment—to collective action—and to himself. As for the loud soldier, he scorns all talk of cowardice. We know nothing more about his attitude.

The youth's problem is still unresolved. As he pursues his "ceaseless calculations," Crane resorts to mathematical terms to make a point, indicating by rational procedures the limitations of the lad's frame of reference. Henry tries, as best he can, to think in "several categories," thereby only increasing the number of divisions in his system of classifications. But only actual experience can bring clarity to his pondering. He will have to "go into the blaze, and then figuratively to watch his legs to discover their merits and faults."

"Blaze, blood, and danger . . . " have to be encountered in battle before Henry can know what his reactions will be. The flaming images Crane uses here may be viewed as symbolic agents of transformation. Blood represents life's energetic powers, which at times must be sacrificed to strengthen one's convictions as in religion or war. The youth will have to encounter actual danger, abandoning his logical approach, in order to find his answer.

Until now he has never known "real" danger; nor did Siegfried or Parzival, for example, until put to the test. Unproven heroes are all "doomed to peace and obscurity." Crane's youth wants to "shine in the war" and to measure himself against the courage of the others. The conflict between a desire for heroism and the possibility of cowardice takes on such proportions that he finds himself in a terrible irresolution. Like a swinging pendulum, he veers from one extreme to another, blaming the unbearable slowness of it all for his unhappiness.

The prolonged waiting ushers in feelings of alienation, of being cut off from other men, who are older and wiser than the youth and come from different backgrounds. He leaves the hut, peers out into the darkness of the night, listens to the trampling feet of the horses as they move about, and sees fleeting shadows in the distance, which he likens to monsters. The noun *monster* (derived from the French verb *montrer*, to reveal or show), indicates the trajectory these fearsome fantasy images must take in order to emerge into the light of consciousness, here the reality of the battlefield.

·When looking out from his encampment across the river, the youth is overcome by a "mystic gloom." The enemy—the unknown—lies on the other side. He stares "at the red eyes" of his antagonists, which seem to grow ever larger and more formidable, and his terror mounts proportionally. He likens them to "the orbs of a row of dragons advancing." The circularity of the "orbs", comparable to a continuous action enclosing upon itself, is identified with the image of the dragon whose terrifying force is associated with the feminine principle. The entire scene gives us a clue to the lad's emotional condition. Let us recall that Siegfried, Perseus, Cadmus, Parzival, St. George, and St. Michael were all dragon-slayers. What they killed, symbolically, was the destructive side of the maternal principle: the chaotic, unregenerate forces within the unconscious. If these are not dealt with, terror may take over, leading to a dissolution of the ego and, concomitantly, insanity.

Now that the youth has stepped out of his hut— that protective inner space—images of eyes, dragons, monsters, and shadows emerge full blown around him. They have become part of the world of contingencies, and their concretion indicates that they are no longer cloistered as amorphous forces in the youth's unconscious. He will have to learn to deal with the inner turmoil that these elemental powers represent, and his emotional growth will depend on the manner in which he stands up to these archetypal forces.

Time passes, and the regiment is finally called upon to march. No action, however, is encountered. During a rest period, the youth lies down on the cool grass and again withdraws into himself. The blades of cool grass "pressed tenderly against his cheek," and he feels Mother Nature's freshness and gentleness—the "liquid stillness of the night enveloping him." He feels in harmony with the cosmos. Then a "vast pity for himself" overcomes him, leading to another regression in which he longs for home, the barn, the cows, the fields, and the security of the farm. He wonders why he had enlisted.

The Initiation into the Patriarchal Fold

Initiation, which requires a forging into subliminal spheres, brings with it an increase in consciousness. This entails the loss of feelings of beatitude, containment, and security, inviting turmoil in the process. To be cast from home into the world of imponderables, as Adam and Eve were when they were ejected from Eden, opens the door to another level of experience: the risk factor. One may flounder, die, or earn redemption and rebirth. During this terrifying period of uncertainty — recalling Christ's battle in the Garden of Gethsemane — primitive depths may be plumbed, vegetative and animal forces penetrated, questions of shame, failure, and fear broached. To kill psychologically what one knows, here the youth's comfortable home condition on the farm, is a prefiguration of the ego's displacement, essential for the birth of a broader and less subjective approach to life. Prior to the youth's enlistment, he was ensconced in the matriarchal fold, but now that he is a member of the army, his relationships are in the process of being reformed on an archetypal level. He is joining the world of the Father, or the patriarchal fold. As in the myths of old, Wolfram von Eschenbach's Parzival in particular, the youth's future development will take place through his encounters with the good or bad offices of certain allegorical figures. Among them are:

The "Loud Soldier"

The "loud soldier," so called because he is filled with bombast at the prospect of destroying the adversary, tells the youth that battle is soon to begin and fills him with war fever. "This time — we'll lick 'em good!" he says, proving himself to be the braggadocio his epithet implies. "How do you know you won't run when the time comes?" the youth questions. Shocked by the audacity of such a thought, the loud soldier asserts that he certainly will fight when the time comes. But still, he has to admit that he does not consider himself "the bravest man in the world." He is annoyed with the youth for posing such an unsettling question. Does he think himself a Napoleon Bonaparte?

The loud soldier's question precipitates further despair on the youth's part. "He felt alone in space," alienated once again from the group, wrestling with "such a terrific problem." He considers himself a "mental outcast," reminiscent of the prophets and saints of old who, like Cain, withdrew into the wilderness to make their covenant with God.

The Dead Soldier

As the youth walks along with his regiment, still deep in thought, he encounters a soldier lying on his back staring at the heavens, with "ashen" face and "dead" eyes and is traumatized at the sight. He shudders as he looks at the mass of inert flesh before him. Feelings of loneliness and isolation increase in the youth, who realizes that this man is cut off from life and nature. "A coldness swept over his back," paralleling the coldness of the opening image of the novel.

Solitude and dissociation make sharp inroads into the youth's psyche as "fierce-eyed" shadows invade the entire area. The enemy is surely ready to strike. Fear imposes itself once again and with it a sense of entrapment. Are the generals competent? he wonders. Do they know what they are doing? Will his regiment be caught in an ambush? Boxed in? Sacrificed because of the leaders' stupidity? Looking at the untested men around him, the youth muses: "They were going to look at war, the red animal—war, the blood-swollen god." How will the soldiers react to this formidable event?

When his brigade finally halts "in the cathedral light of a forest," the youth finds himself once again thrust into nature's fold. The Great Mother's unbridled world of luxuriant vegetable and mineral life lies before his eyes. The image of the "cathedral," superimposed on the obscure and uncultivated wooded area, indicates the need for a religious experience in the form of sublimation of the youth's powerful fear. Religion must be understood here in the Latin sense, *religio*, meaning a linking back, a return to a past time, to an impersonal frame of reference. By regressing in this manner, as previously in the hut, his terrors undergo a depersonalization and objectification process, enabling him to look upon them from a distance.

"It's my first and last battle, old boy," pronounces the loud soldier, who has turned pale. No longer is he outspoken and bombastic, as before the march. When the loud soldier gives him a glance "from the depths of the tomb," the youth understands for the first time that he is not alone. Others also feel fear and anxiety.

Action is at hand. Horses gallop, stragglers stand on the side, shells scream "like a storm banchee," branches break, pounding out their litany of disenchantment. The "battle flag in the distance jerked about madly" as if it is "struggling to free itself from an agony," reminiscent of the banner-shirt image at the beginning of the novel. Smoke and flashes of gunfire pierce the atmosphere — a prefiguration of bloodletting. Thoughts of heroism flicker in the youth's mind as he listens to "the passionate song of the bullets and the banshee shriek of shells."

Crane's visualizations of an army at war are unforgettable. The reader actually hears and sees canon and bullet fire, the moans and agonizing cries of crushed soldiers, the whirling and paralyzing activity of the moment. His use of streaming and strident colors, his slashes of raw, brute verbal pigmentation, add to the harrowing effect of the drama. His depictions take on the authenticity of the sketches of Winslow Homer, who had gone to the front during the Civil War and sent his drawings back to *Harper's Weekly*. His on-the-spot depictions of cavalry officers in combat, infantrymen struck down by bullets, and army life in its crudest manifestations are transmuted by Crane into words. A photographic effect is also discernible in some of the scenes. Like Mathew Brady, the well-known photographer who took some seven-thousand pictures during the height of battle, Crane also features a series of images like black-and-white stills, which lend a gruesome note to his prose depictions of trenches, field hospitals, and rifles lying across dead bodies.[5]

Crane's images of the youth's regiment under constant gunfire—the madness of the wild-eyed men, their faces pale with fear, and the stampeding horses chafing at the bit—are etched in sharp, incisive lines. Blood soaks his pages as rage, chaos, and tumult prevail. The tall soldier loads his rifle as the others run through smoke-infested area, guns clicking, cries cutting the air. The flag, tilted forward, speeds toward the front. Perspiration pours down the youth's face as he peers at the enemy. He fires a wild shot. It's an "automatic affair," he thinks, no longer feeling menaced or even alienated from the other men. On the contrary, he feels a bond to them. To win the war is their only concern. An inner flame has ushered in mysterious feelings of fraternity, as "subtle battle brotherhood" is born of smoke and danger. The youth grows in self-confidence, and rage takes over. He wants to run forward and strangle the enemy with his bare hands. Crane's stunning imagery is reminiscent of Delacroix's canvas, "The Massacre at Scio" (1824), where violence and the magic of color convey the powerful forces clashing in battle.

As the din slackens, the youth's frenzy diminishes and his reason returns. He will wait for the final victory, convinced that the "supreme trial had been passed." Feelings of ecstasy and of self-satisfaction swell within him. At peace with himself, he now knows he is a "fine fellow" after all and he smiles in deep gratification.

Suddenly and without warning, a piercing cry rends the air: the enemy is attacking again. Shells burst and sheets of flame shoot through the air. The flag, "lost in this mass of vapor," may be viewed as a premonitory image of the youth's inner alteration. Crane sees him as a "jaded horse," his "neck quivering with nervous weakness." His feelings of well-being are displaced by terrifying visions of an "onslaught of redoubtable dragons." In contrast to his own fear is the "exalted courage" of the horses as they gallop forward directly into the canon and cavalry fire. Unlike the horses, he runs "like a rabbit" — so shaken is he with terror. He leaps across open fields amid volleys of exploding shells, which take on the countenance of "rows of cruel teeth" grinning at him, ready to chew up his very flesh and fiber. Only when he stops running does he learn that his regiment has held. He cringes in shame. They will discover his failure. He grows angry, not with himself but with his fellow soldiers. He feels "wronged" and "betrayed" by the military as he tries to rationalize his flight. What he did was not only "correct and commendable" but in keeping with common sense. Only his "superior perception and knowledge" caused him to run. Yet, beneath it all, he senses the fallibility of his logic. His walk brings him once again to a forested area. These "dark and intricate places" will cleanse his soul and give him the courage to face his ordeal, as they did for Joseph Conrad's hero in *Heart of Darkness*. In the blackened and secret folds of the Earth Mother, the youth will begin to come to grips with those monstrous pulsations that disturb his inner world.

The Forest Experience

As the sound of shellfire diminishes, Nature appears to the youth in the guise of "a woman with a deep aversion to tragedy," inspiring him with a "religion of peace." No longer amoral, Nature takes on the personality of his own mother, trying to help him out of his quandary. Although he still cannot face his act of cowardice, he feels comforted by what he sees as Nature's approval of his flight. To prove his point, he throws a pine cone "at a jovial squirrel," which causes the animal to run away "with chattering fear." Even a rodent recognizes that one must escape from danger!

He feels freer now that he is convinced—although only superficially—of his natural and prudent act. With greater ease he walks through swamp and under-brush and then reaches a high place where "arching boughs made a chapel." Another experience—we may call it religious—is introduced at this juncture. The youth has not yet come to terms with his gnawing feel-ing of shame.

As he walks toward the "chapel" to find peace with himself, the youth stops dead in his tracks. What he sees is so hideous that he cannot give it a name: "a dead man . . . seated with his back against a columnlike tree." The man's eyes are staring ahead and his mouth is open, its redness having already turned to "an appal-ing yellow;" his ashen-colored face is covered with black ants. Decomposition has already set in.

The youth retreats, turning his back on what might pursue him in his dreams. What really rooted him to the spot, filling him with utter revulsion, was the image of the ants eating away at the corpse's face. His terror becomes paroxysmal as the ants approach the deadman's eyes.

The mood changes as the rustling trees come into sharper focus and begin "softly to sing a hymn of twi-light." The trees communicate to him through the lan-guage of song and lull him into a state of trance. Their harmonies strengthen him, endowing him with feelings that increase his faith in himself. As he hears the shells exploding in the distance and sees the two armies clash-ing, he no longer seeks to withdraw from the fight, but is ready to face the enemy, to make his way out of the forest. In one of Crane's sweeping and macabre ironies, he introduces doggerel into the picture:

> Sing a song 'a 'vic'try,
> A pocketful 'a bullets,
> Five an' twenty dead men
> Baked in a — pie.

Emerging from the forest, the youth joins some soldiers who are marching along with a "tattered man," who is bloodied and dustcovered. A target of derision, the tattered man nevertheless speaks gently in a "girl's voice," his eyes pleading. The youth notices a wound beneath a blood-soaked rag on the man's head and another on his arm, making "that member dangle like a broken bough."

Despite his great pain, the tattered man never complains; he just plods along and tries to start up a conversation. "Was pretty good fight, wa'n't it?" he asks. The youth is so immersed in his own thoughts that he does not hear the question and asks the tattered man to repeat it. Hearing the question finally, he then hurries away. The tattered man catches up with the youth and asks him where he has been hit. Panic seizes the lad and he slides through the crowd, escaping the man who could ferret out his secret and his shame.

But the youth does not feel free — eyes seem to be peering at him. Looking furtively around, he wonders whether "the men were contemplating the letters of guilt he felt burned into his brow." Like the ants eating away at the dead man's eyes, the tattered man, another allegorical figure, forces the youth into a state of self-loathing. Worse, his guilt is now compounded by having deserted the mortally wounded tattered man.

He walks on and comes upon the tall soldier, Jim Conklin, who at the outset of the novel had waved his

shirt bannerlike. Severely wounded, Conklin's features
have taken on a "waxlike" hue. He grabs hold of the
youth's arm and in a "shaking whisper" confesses his
fears, "I tell yeh what I'm, 'fraid of, Henry—I'll tell yeh
what I'm 'fraid of. I'm 'fraid I'll fall down—and 'then
yeh know—them damned artillery wagons—they like
as not 'll run over me. That's what I'm 'fraid of."

The youth cries out that he will care for the tall
soldier, who should not worry. He tries to assure Conklin
of his loyalty as the dying man hangs "babelike to
the youth's arm." Trying to control the sobs that are
overcoming him at the sight of the man's death struggle, the youth falls silent. Despite his loss of blood, the
tall soldier moves off alone into the fields, a "stalking
specter" advancing "with mysterious purpose" into the
distance. The youth follows and then, incredibly, he
hears a soft voice near him. Looking around, he sees
the tattered man who warns him to take the tall soldier
away from this area—a battery of men soon will be
coming along. The tall soldier again pushes forward,
rushing "blindly" into the fields, "running in a staggering and stumbling way toward a little clump of
bushes." Finally, he reaches "the mystic place of his
intentions." As though fulfilling a "solemn ceremony,"
the doomed soldier's movements take on an archetypal
dimension, like the "devotee of a mad religion, blood-
sucking, muscle-wrenching, bone-crunching." The
youth and the tattered man look on in awe, and when
the "doomed soldier begins to heave with a strained
motion," the youth cries out to him once again, offering
his help. As if strengthened by some outerworldly
force, the tall soldier says: "leave me be—don't tech
me—leave me be—." There is silence. The agony is
over. The youth approaches the tall soldier, now lying
lifeless on the ground. He sees an open mouth that
"showed in a laugh," and the side of his body which
appears as "if it had been chewed by wolves." Overcome

with rage, the youth shakes his fist at heaven, which has perpetrated such a giant hoax on man. And in one of the most celebrated similes in the English language, we read: "The red sun was pasted in the sky like a [fierce] wafer."

For Crane, the symbol of the "red sun," like the awarding of the "red badge" of courage, is negative. The word "pasted" suggests artificiality. The fierceness of the hatred aroused in battle and the passivity and amorality of God in His heavens make a mockery of Him and of His Creation. Revealed religion — especially Christianity with its blood communion — is a sham, a giant deception.

The tattered man looks at the dead soldier and praises the courage of this "jim-dandy" fellow. He wonders where he got all that bravery and power to walk on as he did. Then, plodding along the tattered man remarks that the youth looks pretty "pee-ked" and wonders where he is wounded. This is a touchy subject on which the youth is still highly sensitive. Again he grows annoyed. "Oh, don't bother me!" he answers, ready to kill the tattered man for "upraising the ghost of shame on the stick of . . . curiosity." With that he says "good-bye" to the tattered man, who is near death, his speech already slurred and his mind hallucinating. The youth leaves him to wander "about helplessly in the field."

Each time the tattered man asked questions, the youth felt as if a knife had been thrust into him. But knives, swords and cutting instruments are not necessarily death-wielding symbols. They may be positive forces if they cut up problems and rigid points of view, allowing them to be broached in different ways. Here, the lacerating words allow shame — so deeply imbedded within the youth — to surface and be examined from another vantage point. He begins to distinguish the artificial from the authentic, and the egocentric from the fraternal. His rejection of the tattered man forces guilt to emerge as a force with which he will have to contend. That he left this kind person to die alone will haunt the youth for the rest of his days. It will be *his* sin — and he will have to live with it.

Walking on amid the raging battle, he sees death rampant everywhere. He envies the maimed and he weeps, longing to become one of them. He would readily exchange his fate for theirs. He imagines himself blood-soaked and dust-stained, but also courageous in his suffering. A "scorching thirst" comes over him, his bones ache, his feet are like open sores, and he is hungry.

Searching everywhere for his regiment, he hopes it has experienced defeat — a mirror image of his own sense of failure. If that were the case, nobody would know he fled. The regiment would have splintered, each man going his own way, and his flight would be vindicated. More corpses come into view, causing a sharp pang of shame — he longs to be dead, but a hero. If his regiment held the line again, he would be the butt of "shafts" and "derisive grins." The youth questions those around him, but one man, heaving and panting, pushes him away. The youth goes right on with his hysterical questioning: "Why, why . . . ?" Finally, the man, "lurid with rage" takes his rifle and crushes it on the youth's head, who staggers from the pain as "flaming wings of lightning flash before his vision." He then hears a "deafening rumble of thunder" detonating within his head. His "legs seem to die," as he sinks writhing to the ground.

Groaning and writhing, the youth presses his hands to his head. His face is ashen. The battle he fought within himself has now taken on an external dimension. It is the youth's first bout with pain. As he gets up to walk, plagued with anxiety over the depth of his wound, he encounters yet another anguish: the fear of falling. The image of his mother comes to mind — he sees her preparing the meals. The pine walls of the warm kitchen seem to come forward as if to embrace him and the glow of the fire in the stove soothes him.

Suddenly, as if from nowhere, he hears a cheery voice. A stranger begins talking to him about various things—travel, the past. These anecdotes take the youth's mind away from his wound. The stranger's whole attitude is sympathetic and pleasing, proving that here can be a positive and helpful aspect to suffering. With the "wand of magic"—and mirth—the cheery man guides the youth back to his regiment; whistles; and walks away. This allegorical figure with his relaxed, light-hearted ways integrates the youth again into the fraternity of men.

By this time, it is night. Still suffering, the youth realizes he no longer has the strength to invent a fancy tale. He will surely be "a soft target" for the others, but it just does not seem to matter any longer.

"Halt!" shouts a voice from the shadows. It is the loud soldier. Staggering with fatigue, the youth tells him that he was separated from his regiment, that he had a terrible time and was shot. The soldier approaches him with concern and gives him some coffee from his canteen. A corporal approaches and praises the youth's courage. The loud soldier gives him his blanket for the night. The youth stretches out, but then says: "Hol' on a minnit! Where you goin't sleep?" This is the first time he thinks of another person and not exclusively about himself. He finally understands that he is neither better nor worse than the other men in the regiment. They are all made of the same fabric, possessing both courage and cowardice.

Awakening the following morning, the youth feels as if he was asleep for a thousand years. He senses something new: he has passed his initiation. As he looks about, everything appears different to him. Has he experienced a kind of *revelation*? Yes, of sorts. The eastern sky ripples in its splendid array of forms and hues, and the icy dew instills in him a sense of life and vigor. The din of battle is blaring all about, but when the youth hears the sound of those hollow drums and the raw tones of the bugle in the distance, he knows he is entering a new world.

The Rebirth

Still, nobody knows the *real* truth; his comrades think he was wounded in combat. He won't go into details, he decides, still unable to accept his shame. Because he has "performed his mistakes in the dark," he is still considered brave. His new energy inspires him to prove his comrades' opinion of him correct. He takes his rifle, loads it, rushes into the battle, and does his part.

During the course of battle, the youth falls back when forced to yield his position and pushes forward again when possible, fighting with fury and rage. His comrades in arms look at him admiringly; they have now become the spectators that he once was. When the lieutenant observes the youth in the thick of it all "drunk with fighting," he comments: "By heavens, if I had ten thousand wild cats like you I could tear th' stomach out a this war in less 'n a week!" He is a hero, a real devil. During a lull in the fighting, he realizes that after his long night's rest he *awoke a knight.*

As the youth fights on, he hears the "song of the bullets . . . in the air and shells snarled among the tree-tops" and comes to realize that he is "very insignificant." He advances again, but the lieutenant screams at him this time, ordering him to retreat: "Come on, yeh, lunk-head. Come on! We'll al git killed if we stay here." But the youth drives on in a frenzy of action, realizing that something important is at stake: not just his life but the fate of his country. He sees the flag sweeping on in the distance, "glittering," then beginning to falter.

The standard-bearer is wounded but the flag must be protected. "Like a madman," he pushes forward as if propelled by a "despairing fondness for this flag which was near him." He wrenches it out of the clenched fist of the dead standard-bearer, taking for himself this "creation of beauty and vulnerability." The flag is a "goddess, radiant, that bended its form with an imperious gesture to him" and "a woman, red and white, hating and loving, that called him with the voice of his hopes." He dedicates himself to her. No longer a self-indulgent youth, he protects the symbol of his country's ideals. The loud soldier helped him wrench the flag free from the iron grasp of the dead standard-bearer, and together they carry it through the thick and thin of battle.

The flag episode is vital to the youth's psychological evolution. He now knows how he reacts under stress and with this new insight feels at ease in the partriarchal fold. The flag episode also allows him to approach the matriarchate from a different vantage point. The feminine principle is identified with the flag, which he now sees as a protective and unifying power representative of his country's political and social welfare. A kind of totem that embodies the soul of a people, the flag, like the red badge, symbolizes a spiritual as well as an ancestral world. The entire initiation process — and the flag episode is its culmination — makes him conscious of his individuality.

Fierce fighting resumes and again the youth takes part in the "wild battle madness." He and the loud soldier see the enemy's standard-bearer with the "bleach of death" on his face, staggering and then falling. It is the loud soldier's turn to prove his strength. With a mad cry of exultation, he grabs the enemy's flag and knows for himself the meaning of ecstasy. Glorified by their treasures, both the youth and the loud soldier feel wonder, excitement, and fulfillment.

As the fighting subsides, the youth has time to

think back upon his failures and achievements. Shame still lives within him but it lives alongside the remembrance of valorous deeds. With the realization that he is a complex of opposites, he knows he is a *man*.

The youth's days of battle come to a close, "The sultry nightmare was in the past." He looks at the "tranquil skies, fresh meadows, and cool brooks — an existence of soft and eternal peace" and a feeling of serenity comes over him.

The mythic sweep of *The Red Badge of Courage* and the visual and emotional dynamism of its canvases are unique in American literature. The novel went through fourteen printings in its first year. Many critics praised it, but there were also many detractors who criticized its lack of patriotism and egocentric, self-pitying hero. Perhaps Joseph Conrad's words best sum up the depth and scope of Crane's achievement. This is the work of "an artist," he writes, "of a man not of experience but a man inspired, a seer with a gift for rendering the significant on the surface of things and with an incomparable insight into primitive emotions, who, in order to give us the image of war, had looked profoundly into his own breast."[6]

4

George's Mother

Although, in Hamlin Garland's opinion, *Maggie* was "a work of astonishingly good style, pictorial, graphic, terrible in its directness," it only dealt with the worst elements of slum life. Crane should broaden his vision, he advised, to include the world of those "who live lives of heroic purity and hopeless hardship."[1] Crane took Garland's suggestions seriously when composing *George's Mother*, his second novel dealing with slum life. It "leaves *Maggie* at the post," Crane wrote. "It is my best thing."[2]

Crane returned to the Bowery for inspiration for *George's Mother*. After the failure of *Maggie*, this indicates either a certain amount of self-confidence or foolhardiness on his part. The success of *The Red Badge of Courage* gave Crane cause for elation. The reviews, as previously noted, were stunningly favorable for the most part. Harold Frederic, the American writer and London correspondent of the *New York Times*, wrote a glowing review, "Stephen Crane's Triumph," which praised the young writer for his thematic and structural innovations. Crane's return to the Bowery for his next novel perhaps may be explained by an urgent inner need to deal with certain autobiographical material. The mother in *George's Mother* perhaps was modeled on Crane's own and there is also a bit of Stephen Crane in George.

Whatever his reasons for choosing another Bowery setting, Crane felt confident of the authenticity of his fiction. His descriptions of the neighborhood and the people have the accuracy of a photograph. He also used color to heighten situations and to dramatize personali-

ties. Whether he had read or only heard of Goethe's
Theory of Colors (1810, English trans., 1840) is unknown,
but, in accordance with that work, he used vibrant
greens, reds, brilliant blues, silvers, and burning yel-
lows to underscore vigorous and vociferous encounters
and ashen or dull tones for passive or deathlike episodes. In keeping with Goethe's dictum: "Experience
teaches us that particular colors excite particular states
of feeling," Crane assigned an aesthetic and emotional
value to every color. He interpolated color into the very
fabric of his prose, into its structure, rhythms, and
figures of speech. Examples are the metaphors of
"crimson roar," the epithet "grey paste" for a dying man,
the symbol of "red mittens."[3] Bowery life allowed Crane
to use his palette to describe a milieu rife with corruption — the opium addict, the alcoholic, the pimp, and
the prostitute — as well as the honor and idealism of the
police force.

Less allegorical and more personal than his former
novels, *George's Mother* focuses on the conflict between a
church-going, temperance-adhering woman, Mrs. Kelcey, bereft of her husband and four of her five sons, and
George, her single remaining offspring. Although all
her energies are centered on him, George neither lives
up to her expectations nor fulfills his own visions. Since
he is the paradigm of the anti-hero and the antithesis of
Horatio Alger, he differs from St. George, his namesake, who slew the dragon. Crane's George is a solipsis-
tic dreamer. Weakly structured and naive, he is so opposed to his mother's single-purposed mind that no
possible communication can exist between them. Each
lives in a closed world, obsessed with what he or she
believes to be the *right* way.

The action is condensed into a short timespan. By
using principally a third-person point of view to relate
the events and by alluding to his characters by means of
epithets, Crane gains objectivity, becoming the eye that
peers into the heart of his creations. Devoid of senti-

mentality and moralizing, the novel presents sharp, stark, and unembellished characters.

Mrs. Kelcey was partly modeled, as has been stated, on Crane's mother. The author always thought it inconceivable that his mother, Helen Peck, an intelligent university graduate who wrote for magazines and journals, could devote her life almost exclusively to church activities and to temperance: "the vacuous, futile, psalm-singing that passed for worship."[4] Religion, particularly after her husband's death, was always her greatest solace. Although Crane rebelled against this implacable woman—sometimes brutally—he was, strangely enough, fascinated by her vibrant inner force. George inherits some of the author's ambivalent love-hate feelings for his mother.

Critics like to point to Zola's *Dram Shop* as being influential in Crane's detailed depiction of the evils of alcohol. Although this influence may exist, it is well to recall that saloon literature had flooded the American market beginning in the middle of the nineteenth century. Walt Whitman's *Franklin Evans or The Inebriate* (1842) sketched the vicious and degrading effects of drink, as did T. S. Arthur's *Ten Nights in a Barroom* and its sequel, *Three Years in a Man Trap* (1872). Edgar Fawcett's *A Man's Will* (1888) was also a melodramatic vision of stunted lives filled with shame, poverty, and sickness, their degradation due to "spirits." Even Crane's father, Reverend Jonathan Townley Crane, had written *Arts of Intoxication* (1870), a work that encouraged those who had lost themselves in the evils of smoke and drink to recover their self-respect and thereby earn redemption.

The Swirling Rain

George's Mother, like *The Red Badge of Courage*, opens with a stunning tableau of nature aroused: "In the swirling rain that came at dusk the broad avenue glistened with that deep bluish tint which is so widely condemned when it is put into pictures." The "swirling rain" provides a premonitory image that hints at the confusion of the emotions that will soon surface. It is significant that the action begins at "dusk" as a world of shadows comes to the fore, representing the forces that lurk in the unconscious of Crane's protagonists. Emerging every now and then, these forces inflict pain and cruelty upon the undiscerning and naive. That the avenue "glistened" indicates the brilliance and allure of the collective domain, or the outside world, which dazzles and captivates. Juxtaposed with the "golden light" of the many shops on the avenue is the "deep bluish tint" that adds to the darkness of the scene, increasing the power of those eerie phantomlike creatures roaming about in the recesses of the mind. The rain that beats down dampens the spirits but also has a cleansing effect, wiping away surface grime that could obstruct a clear view of people and events.

Crane's fertile imagination allows him to compare the massive buildings in this slum to medieval "castles and fortresses," thereby removing them from their contemporary setting and embedding them in the eternity of history. Stonelike, impenetrable, and harsh, the solid, jagged buildings stand in this modern walled city, protecting its spiritual and cultural powers from destruction. By the same token, they also maintain and foster repressive, entangling, and disturbing alliances, which may be considered as unsifted or undetermined primal forces.

George is first seen as he walks along the street, a lunch pail under his arm and a corn-cob pipe between his lips. He meets a friend, Charley Jones, whom he hasn't seen since the previous year when they both had moved from the country to the city. Jones invites him to a "little glass-fronted saloon that sat blinking jovially at the crowds." A personification of the pleasure principle, the saloon, representing joy and delight, is looked upon with welcome relief by George whose life is humdrum and austere. After drinking a few glasses of beer, George rushes home, fearing his mother might be worrying about him.

The Dragon Lady

There is a change of scene. We hear the hymnlike song of an "old voice" that "quavered and trembled," comparable to "a sound-spirit" that "had a broken wing." We then see that the woman in question is by no means frail. She is the antithesis of Whistler's mother as she wields her pots, pans, brooms, and dust-pan like "weapons." Indeed, they are instruments of battle for the struggle taking place in the heart of the matriarchal world. The rigid, autocratic, ascetic Mrs. Kelcey is the power within the fortress:

There was the flurry of a battle in this room. Through the clouded dust or stream one could see the thin figure dealing mighty blows. Always her way seemed beset. Her broom was continually poised, lance wise, at dust demons. There came clashings and clangings as she strove with her fireless foes.

The alliterations in the above quotation highlight Mrs. Kelcey's strength and vigor. Like a medieval hero, she is endowed with a fighting spirit, capable of annihilating the demons around her by purifying the atmosphere. Faith and willpower keep her going. Though her voice may have trembled while singing, "it was often raised in a long cry, a strange war-chant, a shout of battle and defiance, that rose and fell in harsh screams."

The old woman's arch enemy is an "enormous brewery" that "towered over the other buildings" in the distance with its "great gilt letters" which "advertised a brand of beer." A "stupendous affair, a machine of mighty strength," this dangerous antagonist looms larger than life. Unlike Mrs. Kelcey's voice, which is compared to "a sound-spirit" with a "broken wing," the factory is identified with "a great bird," the size of a vulture. There is no end, it seems, to the heights it can reach or to the poisons it can distill. An instrument of perdition, the organizational power of this inhuman force has to be stopped. The mother's battle against the brewery, enacted on a spiritual level, is like her daily attempt to battle with brooms and dust pans the ever-increasing scourge of dust and grime that comes through her open windows. Like Sisyphus, who pushed the stone up the mountain by day only to find that it had rolled down during the night, Mrs. Kelcey pursues her futile task with vigilance and perseverance. "Terrific blows were given and received. There arose the clattering uproar of a new fight. The little intent warrior never hesitated nor faltered. She fought with a strong relentless will."

Crane compares Mrs. Kelcey to a "dragon," thereby linking her forcefully with the medieval castle and fortress images. It is Mrs. Kelcey's dragon-aspect that attacks George on another occasion when he returns home late from a drinking evening with Jones. "On the verge of tears," she reprimands him for his tardiness and orders him to hang up his coat behind the door — a command she repeats nearly every evening. Her order takes on the proportions of an unpleasant ritual for George. He is so accustomed to her commands that he no longer hears them. They have become routine and meaningless. For Mrs. Kelcey, however, a principle is at stake. She wants her son to lead an *ordered* life, and hanging up a coat when returning from work is a manifestation of orderliness.

George tells his mother he was out with Jones, and her reaction is automatic and mechanical: "I don't like him." He then confronts her: how could she not like Jones to whom she has never even spoken? She retreats before his aggressive tone but still argues the point. We realize now that she considers destructive, and rejects, anything that separates her from her son — be it lateness or any other entanglement.

After George "wandered aimlessly through the meal," his mother asks him to accompany her to a prayer meeting, coaxing him into surrender by putting her arms around his neck and using all the wiles at her disposal to enforce her will. The thought of this solemn and "blackening" religious experience vexes George, particularly after the warmth and conviviality of his afternoon escapade. Hurt by his refusal to go, the mother puts on her shawl and, casting "a martyr-like glance" at her son, exits, looking like "a limited funeral procession." George finds release from his guilt-dominated world by kicking the leg of the kitchen table. That he has to resort to such secret ways of fighting back indicates the weakness of his ego and his inability to face either himself or this dragonlike force.

The Cheery Bar

Soon after his mother leaves, George returns to the cheery bar to drink and relax with Jones and other habitués. No bickerings, no reprimands, no antagonisms. George admires Jones for his "great eloquence and wit." He also discovers his own remarkable potential. "He was capable of sublime things," he thinks, and pictures himself "magnificent in his friendship." For the first time he understands the meaning of "fraternal" feelings. These hours spent with Jones and his friends, he is now convinced, are the happiest in his life.

George arrives home late that night. When his mother awakens him the next morning, he is still drowsy. "Damn these early hours," he says, knowing that swearing is anathema to her. His words have the impact of a "missile" flung her way, and the terrain is vulnerable to attack. Certainly he must have been out drinking, she remarks accusingly. To churn the blade in the wound, she contrasts his sordid character with the lofty ways of his father and brothers. Only as George is about to leave for work does she retreat from full-fledged battle, becoming "meek" and conciliatory. "Ain't yeh goin' t' kiss me good-by," she asks woefully. With the "dignity of an injured monarch who plays the battle scene with astuteness," George makes believe he has not heard his mother's request, forcing her to pose the question again, whereupon he kisses her with tenderness.

Mrs. Kelcey's love and admiration for her son fills the vacuum caused by other family misfortunes. She creates illusions about him. He was late, not because of drinking but rather the suffering brought on by "a great internal disease. It was something no doubt that devoured the kidneys or quietly fed upon the lungs." A woman must have been involved—"wicked and fair," like those fascinating chatelaines of old who inhabited fortresses and castles.

George's mood changes for the better after the night of the quarrel. He "made a show of waltzing with [his mother] so that she spilled some of the coffee." For an entire week George returns home, as he always has, in time for dinner; then he reads his paper and smokes his pipe. Mrs. Kelcey is convinced that all is well again; "that she was a perfect mother, rearing a perfect son." George also sees himself through his mother's eyes and believes he is "the most marvellous young man on earth." Since ambivalence frequently accompanies such mother/son relationships, savage emotions also ruminate in his mind. He feels hatred for this stern, rigid, unbending woman who forces him into a state of sub- servience. An unbreachable chasm exists between them, and each stagnates behind walls of illusion. Though this state is dangerous for the mother, it is more so for the son, who has not yet discovered his groundbed or carved out his future.

The Dream Girl

George's encounter with Jones opens a new *way* for him to discover the mysteries of the big city. It also activates his imagination, enticing him into living out what had formerly existed only as a fantasy image. Some "indefi- nite woman" is always running after him in his dreams, consumed with a "wild, torrential passion for him." That he always reacts to his "dream-girl", to this "peer- less woman's love" in an "icy, self-possessed" manner is considered admirable by friends and neighbors, with whom he discusses his fantasies. One day his fantasy will be fulfilled. Of this he is certain. He merely has to wait for the right time. He and the woman of his fancy will move into a royal existence: wild lands, servants, horses, and elegant elegant clothes. Self-indulgent and unrealistic, he lives with goddesses and chariots in a world of billowing pink clouds.

George's fantasy images become reality when he sees Maggie Johnson, who lives in his tenement, walk- ing up the stairs carrying a pail of beer. She is his ideal. Her look of utter indifference does not stop him from hoping to place "her in the full glory of that sun." In time, she becomes "the goddess, pitched from her ped- estal," who "lay prostrate, unheeded, save when he brought her forth to call her insipid and childish in the presence of this new religion." He views himself as hero and savior. Why else would he have been born, were it not to play out this role? Soon his power over Maggie will become evident to all. His dreams, however, are dashed when a young man on his way to visit Maggie asks him to direct him to the Johnson apartment. George is furious.

George's reaction to his disappointment is both melodramatic and infantile. Upon reaching his apartment, Mrs. Kelcey tells him to hang up his jacket on the hook behind the door. He explodes, turning toward his mother with hate and rage. Unable to deal with his emotions, he releases his anger on a scapegoat—kicking a table as before and screaming at his mother. Now a wall of silence is built again between Mrs. Kelcey and her son, and battle lines are drawn. As she retreats to her room, her hip strikes against the corner of the table. Moments later, she closes the door and all paths of communication are closed.

During the days that follow, George is depressed, not an uncommon condition for someone shocked into recognizing the reality of his situation. When Jones again invites him to a saloon, he accepts with pleasure, hoping to glide out of his moroseness as rapidly as he had slipped into it. Under the influence of alcohol, he finds himself reaching out into life and entering into a fine and thrilling world, relieved of his mother's austerity.

As Jones and George imbibe increasing quantities of liquor. a sense of elation comes over them. Jones grabs George in a fit of merriment, and the two waltz around the floor until they both fall down. More is drunk, and George becomes obstreperous. His erstwhile friends bury him under a heap of chairs and tables.

George awakens hours later to a saloon that resembles a "decaying battle-field:" overturned chairs, tables, broken tumblers, and bottles. He feels hurt all over, physically as well as psychologically. Former friends, who fell from grace, are like primordial beings, each taking on giant proportions, surpassing human stature in power and strength. He feels dwarfed in their presence, devoured and strangled by the very forces he tries to equal and surpass. Unwilling to accept a tarnished image of himself, George quickly casts a negative eye upon his drinking partners: they are sinful and weak, not he. His feelings of contempt for them help George to face the world once again.

When George does not arrive home on the night of his drinking bout, his frantic mother goes the following day to see the foreman of the shop where her son is employed. She inquires if George was at work, and the answer is no. George is home by the time she returns. There was an accident, he explains. A pole was struck by a truck and fell on him, knocking him unconscious. He was hospitalized and returned home directly after his release. When his mother asks him to accompany her to a prayer meeting that night, George complies. Rather than feeling inspired and uplifted by the prayers and sermon he hears, he is overwhelmed by a sense of damnation and censure. He is a pariah, cut off from others. Several nights later, his mother again asks him to join her and her friends, but George refuses. She resorts to her usual weapon: the reprimand. Still he says no, but she persists. Finally, in desperation, he throws down his paper and harshly asks to be left alone.

The more George feels entrapped, the angrier he becomes and the greater his need for Jones and his friends to fight the dragon at home and within himself. Since the terrible night of his humiliation, however, George has sought other friends, hoping to find release with them, though these are no longer good fellows but neighborhood hoodlums. One of them even whipped his employer and, considering his act a show of courage, was proud of his achievement. Their values are different from George's: to work is not only considered

futile but cowardly. On one occasion, George joins
forces with them and helps them catch and punish one
of their antagonists. His bravura during the altercation
is in keeping with his new friends' ethics and rouses
their admiration. But in time illusions are deflated on
both sides.

George's late hours make it difficult for him to
awaken in the morning and to go to work. But his
mother, nevertheless, perseveres, calling out in her
"shrill voice" for him to get up. So angry is he one
morning that a cascade of obscenities gushes from his
mouth. For three days mother and son do not speak to
each other. George feels an unfamiliar and singular
pleasure in his mother's "agony," her humiliation com-
pensation for his own frustrations. Some days later he
tells his mother he has been fired. She becomes ill, and
his reaction is not one of concern but of annoyance. He
feels deprived of that exquisite revenge he hoped to take
on her. As he observes the pallor spreading over her
face, he is overcome with feelings of thanksgiving. Never suspecting his covert feelings of hatred toward her,
she smiles calmly and denies being sick, not wanting to
cause her son any worry.

The Chamber of Death

George's alcoholism worsens, as does his mother's illness. Neighbors come to the apartment to help clean
and cook. The inevitable finally occurs. When George
enters "the chamber of death," he walks toward the old
woman and calls "Mother—mother," speaking with reverence "lest this mystic being upon the bed should
clutch at him." Mrs. Kelcey, however, no longer recognizes her son. She lives in the past when her husband
and children were young and life seemed to shine upon
her. As she retreats from this world, she calls out in

anguish, "Help me! Help me!" Monsters people her world now with such force and amplitude that the Church itself, in the form of the plump clergyman tending her, cannot fend them off. Her faith, which once consoled her, brings her no solace. To George, the clergyman utters his condolences in the most artful and mechanical of ways—a master in the automatism of his long-practiced trade. "My poor lad," he says.

George's Mother was praised by William Dean Howells for its tempered realism, its artistry, and the "compassion" Crane showed toward "everything that errs and suffers." H. L. Mencken criticized Crane's "method," which he considered "grossly ill-adapted to the novel" since it lacked any "literary small talk," but praised Crane's "superlative skill" and "dazzling brilliance." Garland was disappointed. *George's Mother*, will "live only as a literary phase of a brilliant young literary man." Edward Garnett, in the *London Academy*, considered it a masterpiece:

"An ordinary artist would seek to dive into the mind of the old woman, to follow its workings hidden under the deceitful appearance of things. . . . A great artist would so recreate her life that its griefs and joys became significant of the griefs and joys of all motherhood on earth. But Mr. Crane does neither. He simply reproduces the surfaces of the individual life in as marvelous a way that the manner in which the old woman washes up the crockery, for example, gives us to her. To dive into the hidden life is, of course, for the artist a great temptation and a great danger—the values of the picture speedily get wrong, and the artist, seeking to interpret life, departs from the truth of nature. The rare thing about Mr. Crane's art is that he keeps closer to the surface than any living writer, and, like the great portrait-painters, to a great extent makes the surface betray the depths.[5]

5

The Third Violet

"The high dramatic key of *The Red Badge of Courage* cannot be sustained," Crane wrote about *The Third Violet*, the novel he began in 1895. In contrast to his powerful war book, he saw his new endeavor as "a quiet little story," and his assessment of *The Third Violet* was indeed perceptive.[1]

The Third Violet, which contains autobiographical elements, tells the story of Billie Hawker who falls in love with Miss Fanhall, a wealthy and aristocratic young lady. The authenticity of the country and city scenes is unquestionable. Crane modeled the former on the Hartwood landscape where his brother Edmund had a home and on a guest camp in Pike's County, Pennsylvania where he had spent a summer. As for the sections featuring Hawker's life as an artist in New York City, they, too, were based on experience. Crane moved in with painter friends in 1894. Drinking, smoking, and playing poker with them, he listened to their dreams and illusions. He also had read and heard about works describing the artist's world: Richard Harding Davis's "A Patron of Art" (1892), Robert W. Chambers's *In the Quarter* (1894), and Howells's *A Hazard of New Fortunes* (1890) and *The Coast of Bohemia* (1893). As for Miss Fanhall, Hawker's great love, she, too, may have been modeled on Helen Trent and Lily Brandon Munroe.

Despite Crane's intimacy with artists and their

mode of life and his understanding of human nature, the characters in *The Third Violet* seem inauthentic, stereotypical. Uninteresting and unreal, they are as awkward as wooden puppets, entering and exiting from a setting of contrived situations. The dialogue is sophomoric, melodramatic, and waxes platitudes. Moreover, the entire novel sounds like a reportage. What could have been sequences of vibrant, electrifying interludes are nothing but stale encounters and uninspiring incidents that have no impact. What remains unforgettable in *The Third Violet*, however, are Crane's visualizations of machines and of nature, his depictions of people silhouetted against an open sky or sharply delineated in various poses, and also his moving depictions of animals.

The Black Monster

The opening of *The Third Violet* takes on the power of an apocalyptic vision. It features a "black monster"—a metaphor for a train—that may be looked upon as a premonitory image of the painful love episodes to be dramatized. The black monster arrives at the small country station, released its passengers who burst forth with the enthusiasm of convicts set free. Within the train, representing the constrictions of city life and all ties and bonds, are contained the freedom-seekers: those in need of fresh air or fresh approaches to life.

The reader is first introduced to the protagonists in this little country station: Billie Hawker, a poor painter who returns to his hometown to visit his family of hardworking farmers; wealthy Miss Grace Fanhall, beautiful and charming; her sister-in-law and her children who will spend a few weeks at the elegant resort hotel. Hawker is immediately and intensely drawn to Miss Fanhall—his ideal of womanhood. During their stagecoach ride, Hawker looks at this vision of loveliness: "fleeting glances of a cheek, an arm, or a shoulder." But Hawker does not see her *whole*. As in a Cubist découpage, only parts of this fantasy image are visible to him. Unlike others of her social class, Miss Fanhall is unaffected and warm, but Hawker feels socially inferior to her. Whenever he approaches her, his speech and his mannerisms become awkward, stilted, and self-conscious. Their conversations make him appear—he feels—"perfectly ridiculous." While she is at ease with him, he is not with her because of his deeply embedded sense of inferiority. He is so intent on creating a favorable impression, it is impossible for him to do so. Perceptive and sensitive to his feelings, Miss Fanhall cannot but chide him for his own class prejudices.

Animals, Silhouettes, Nature

Outstanding in this comedy of manners are Crane's extraordinary depictions of animals and his empathetic approach to nature. Certain sections must be singled out for their depth, perception, and beauty of feeling.

After the stagecoach ride, Hawker arrives at his parents' home in the country and his dog, Stanley, comes out to greet him. The animal's joyous reactions are so exuberantly portrayed that only someone who knows dogs could have captured the intensity of Stanley's antics:

The ardor for battle was instantly smitten from the dog and his barking swelled in a gurgle of delight. He was a large orange and white setter and he partly expressed his emotion by twisting his body into a fantastic curve and then dancing over the ground with his head and his tail very near to each other. He gave vent to little sobs in a wild attempt to vocally describe his gladness.

Crane evokes the dog's feelings through image, rhythm, and sensory impressions. So real, vibrant, and effective is the outcome, that the reader feels as if he were sharing in this marvelously happy greeting.

Crane's studies of "middle-aged ladies of the most aggressive respectability," sitting on the porch of the fashionable country club, take on the precision and incisiveness of a Daumier caricature and the depth of a Hogarth etching. Crane, like these artists, sees into human beings and reaches down to their deepest natures. Unsparing in his assessment of people's malice, he draws them in hard, piercing lines. His contempt for them is commensurate with theirs for others.

The women silhouetted so provocatively by Crane return to the hotel every year; they make up one-third of the summer guests. Their purpose, remarks Crane, is to sit on the "porch and take measurements of character as authoritatively as if they constituted the jury of heaven." With satire and irony, he describes the shallowness of their ideas and their puritanical mentality. Contemptible in their need for gossip, these so-called paragons of virtue are in reality human scavengers seeking out the sorrows of others to feed their empty lives.

Nature takes on added excitement under Crane's brush strokes and pigmentations, as, for example, in Hawker's boatride with Miss Fanhall:

The wind swept from the ridge top where some great bare pines stood in the moonlight. A loon called in its strange unearthly note from the lake shore. As Hawker turned the boat toward the dock, the flaring rays from the moon fell upon the head of the girl in the rear seat and he rowed very slowly.

Crane's sense of form and his elliptical, polished style are reminiscent of a similar boat scene in Henry James's *The Ambassadors*. In both instances, the outer world takes on a variety of precisely rendered colors. Instead of the usual classical, fixed, even rigid approach to nature, the reader here, and in James's novel, is offered a landscape of suggestive wonder.

When on another occasion Hawker takes his easel into the fields, we are immersed in the wonder of the outdoors: "In a wood the light sifted through the foliage and burned with a peculiar reddish lustre on the masses of dead leaves." In a splendid personification, a little brook is bursting with vigor and life: "a brawling, ruffianly little brook, swaggered from side to side down the glade, swirling in white leaps over the great dark rocks and shouting challenge to the hillsides." The reader feels the water on his body, hears it splashing about, and may experience a sense of purification and renewal.

One of the most unforgettable tableaux in *The Third Violet* is the scene in which Hawker and Miss Fanhall walk through the fields and come upon the artist's father who is driving his team of oxen:

Presently a team of oxen waddled into view around the curve of the road. They swung their heads slowly from side to side, blended under the yoke and looking out at the world with their great eyes in which was a mystic note of their humble, submissive, toilsome lives. An old wagon creaked after them and erect upon it was the tall and tattered figure of the farmer swinging his whip and yelling: "Whoa!-haw there! Git-ap!" The lash flicked and flew over the broad backs of the animals.

Hawker is embarrassed by what he considers to be his socially inferior family background. Unconsciously, he contrasts the wealth of the urban socialite and his own humble means, Miss Fanhall's cultured manners and his father's crude ways. He feels distinctly ill at ease, but Miss Fanhall, not a bit condescending, is delighted by the fun of it all. She relates to the artist's father and is charmed by the animals. She asks if she can have a ride in the cart. The father agrees, and the two "become so absorbed in their conversation that they seemed to forget the painter."

In this and in other settings which fix nature's riches, Crane's idyllic and glowing visions are reminiscent not so much of the canvases of the French impressionist painters as they are of the less well-known group of artists, who made their home in Barbizon not far from Paris. Corot, Rousseau, Daubigny, Millet, and others underscored the elusive side of meandering brooks, haystacks, hills, fields, misty slopes, and gently forested areas. They knew just how to transmute a blue sky glimpsing through foliage into gently muted tones. Light seemed to vibrate for these artists as it did verbally for Crane, shedding an array of exquisite tonalities over entire canvases. Crane's forms and contours are composed of small particles of exciting shadings and nuances.

The Bohemian

After Miss Fanhall's return to an elegant neighborhood in New York City and Hawker's to a poor artist's garret studio, the natural spontaneity of country life gives way to the culturally stratified city, which seems to be composed of two antithetical worlds.

Hawker's Bohemian world was modeled, as mentioned above, on Crane's life with a group of artists or art students ("indians," he called them) in an old building on East Twenty-third Street. According to his acridly humorous description of their doings, they all slept on the floor, dined on buns and sardines, and painted on towels or wrapping paper for lack of canvas. He complained of the noise and confusion of these "savages, all dreaming blood-red dreams of fame."[2] Somehow his descriptions of their joys and sorrows do not ring true; they are shallow and overdone. Romance and bohemianism, as depicted in Eugène Sue's *The Mysteries of Paris* (1842–43) and in Henry Murger's *Scenes of Bohemian Life* (1848), to mention only two, had worn thin. There was little new that could be said through realism about the romantics. Crane's characters with their scarce of food and beautiful models *are* intriguing, but they are simply not new. Their lives and conversations seem hackneyed. Even his description of their studio is an unoriginal recreation of the working quarters of one of America's great artists, Albert Pinkham Ryder, whom Crane had met:

> dull walls lined with sketches, the tousled bed in one corner, the masses of boxes and trunks in another, a little dead stove, and the wonderful table. Moreover, there were wine-coloured draperies flung in some places, and on a shelf, high up, there were plaster casts, with dust in the creases. There were some elaborate cobwebs on the ceiling.

In Lewis Mumford's *The Brown Decades*, Ryder's studio is seen in almost the same manner: "A mere litter of tables, chairs, trunks, packing boxes, old magazines and newspapers, dirty cups and dishes on the floor, with stale food still left on them, the long streamers of paper hanging from the ceiling, dust and cobwebs everywhere."[3]

Crane seemingly was collecting bits and pieces of information here and there and inserting them into his work when he had to fill out empty spots, the result being a certain shallowness and choppiness in the flow of ideas.

Characterizations and Plot

Crane's characterizations also were not innovative. Neither unaffected Miss Fanhall nor nervous Hawker take on life. Both characters are paper cut-outs, intellectual constructs. Even Hawker's gaucheness, to which he freely admits, is sham. He keeps emphasizing, much to her annoyance, that Miss Fanhall is an heiress. The reader, aware of this fact from the start, will find her repeated illusions quite monotonous. Always having lived a charmed existence, she finds Hawker's world attractive, actually seeing it as romantic. For her it spells diversity and excitement. She does not scorn him when he talks about his poverty and the fact that even after having studied art in Paris he must paint corn and asparagus on can covers to earn his living. Nor does she consider commercial art a disgrace. She appreciates him for the talent *she* lacks.

Crane's plot is not distinctive either. The three violets, which give the novel its title, have, for some critics, a symbolic value in that they indicate fidelity in love. The first of the violets, which Miss Fanhall drops accidentally on the tennis court in the country, was to be a memento for Hawker; she gives him the second in the most natural of ways but accompanied by such a mannered speech that he is unable to understand the feelings behind the gift. He concludes rashly that their relationship must end and later goes to her elegant New York City home to say goodby. At this point, she offers him a third violet. He exclaims, "Please don't pity me" — a self-indulgent remark that angers the young girl. "Oh, do go! Please! I want you to go!" she tells him with tears in her eyes. Hawker realizes for the first time that she is spontaneous and sincere, and even though Miss Fanhall quickly recovers her self-control, those seconds of anger give Hawker joy and hope. No longer does he despair. And the novel concludes: "Later, she told him that he was perfectly ridiculous."

When Crane sent *The Third Violet* to his publisher, he thought it might not be accepted because it lacked "the sting it would have if written under the spur of pain."[4] After its publication, Richard Harding Davis wrote that "In England nothing succeeds like success. Mr. Crane, one would think, would be the first to confess that his last little book, *The Third Violet*, is an absolutely unpretentious piece of work." Also H. G. Wells was critical:

it is not a successful demonstration, that Crane could write a charming love story. It is the very simple affair of an art student and a summer boarder, with the more superficial incidents of their petty encounters set forth in a forcible, objective manner that is curiously hard and unsympathetic. The characters act, and on reflection one admits they act, *true*, but the play of their emotions goes on behind the curtain of the style, and all the enrichments of imaginative appeal that make love beautiful are omitted.[5]

6

Active Service

Is *Active Service* a parody or sentimental potboiler or a combination of both? If it is a spoof, mocking the popular romances and adventure stories of the day, then it is hugely funny and smartingly caustic. Since the plot is absurd, the protagonists superficial and overdrawn, the climaxes incredible, and the dialogue hackneyed, Crane indeed may have been parodying the stereotypical, treating serious subjects in a nonsensical way. *Active Service* also may be seen as a caricature of the romances written by writers such as Sir Walter Scott and Alexandre Dumas. Contrived situations materialize without rhyme or reason. The characters escape danger miraculously. Also ridiculed are the Gothic mysteries with their eerie situations, their vamps sinking their fangs into their prey, their beautiful but vacuous young girls, who are no longer chatelaines on a medieval estate, but now the daughters of Ivy League college professors.

If, however, we look upon *Active Service* merely as a conventional novel, Crane seems caught up in the manneristic tradition: staged melodramatic sequences and a parasitic identification with his hero's adventures in a variety of bathetic situations. If the latter is the case, *Active Service* is not worthy of inclusion in an analysis of his works. The former appraisal, however, is opted for here.

Mannerist Satire

Active Service revolves around the Greco-Turkish War of 1897. From the very outset, readers know they are encountering melodramatic, high-tension passion, typi-

cal of the manneristic novel that was so popular in the
nineteenth century.

Marjory Wainwright, the daughter of a professor
at Washurst College, is first seen walking "pensively
along the hall" to her father's study. "In the cold shadows made by the palms of the window edge, her face
wore the expression of thoughtful melancholy expected
of the faces of the devotees who pace in cloistered
gloom." We seem to be in the heart of the Gothic novel,
as attention is focused on a young, naive, tender-
hearted girl, whose life seems eclipsed by a harrowing
march of events. Pain and suffering will certainly be
hers. Perhaps she is also the literary offspring of a
beautiful and wistful Scott or Bronte heroine? The
reader expects a knight in shining armor to appear,
take her in his arms and sweep her off to some Edenic
place. Or will it be a devilish, sinister being who will
hold her captive in some shadowy realm? Crane, a
devotee of medieval and Renaissance lore, underscores
Marjory's ultrapassionate nature. Nevertheless, this
wistful, well-bred, and refined girl follows the dictates
of her social class and acts with restraint under all circumstances.

As the deeply distressed Marjory enters her father's office, she interrupts this "great" scholar at work.
He is annoyed by the intrusion. What could she have in
mind? he wonders. Certainly, it will be of no importance, merely some trivial matter. Crane digs deeply
into the father's character, mocking the stereotypical
objects to be found in the study, which include a "bust
of Pericles on the mantel." Also mocked is the professor's pedantry, which is exemplified in his sententious
writing style:

one of his sentences, ponderous, solemn and endless, in
which wandered multitudes of homeless and friendless prepo-
sitions, adjectives looking for a parent, and quarreling

nouns, sentences which no longer symbolized the language form of thought but which had about them a quaint aroma from the dens of long-dead scholars."

Professor Wainwright shoos his daughter away. He is in the midst of important work—he is writing!

Crane's delineation of the professor's writing style conveys his reaction to the aridity of the scholar who considers his thoughts and predictions of utmost importance. He evaluates the professor's writing style as a motley combination of rhetorical devices used to blacken paper, a means of impressing students and colleagues with the weight of pseudo-knowledge, and as pedantic, sense-dulling intellectual meanderings.

Crane harps on Professor Wainwright's intellectual pursuits with stunning verity, perhaps ridding himself of his own spleen against those boring professors whose classes he had cut at Claverack, Lafayette, and Syracuse:

A man focused upon astronomy, the pig-market or social progression, may nevertheless have a secondary mind which hovers like a spirit over his dahlia tubers and dreams upon the mystery of their slow and tender revelations. The professor's secondary mind had dwelt always with his daughter and watched with faith and delight the changing to a woman of a certain fat and mumbling babe. However, he now saw this machine, this self-sustained, self-operative love, which had run with the ease of a clock, suddenly crumble to ashes and leave the mind of a great scholar staring at a calamity.

The self-righteous scholar listens to his distressed daughter inform him of her plan to marry the journalist, Rufus Coleman, Sunday Editor of the *New York Eclipse*. At first upset by this outrageous bit of news, the staid father then begins to grow apprehensive. He feels a pang of guilt. He has never devoted any time to his family, letting it be understood that he preferred burying himself in books and living a life of the mind. The explanation of his preference lies in the personality of Mrs. Wainwright: she is an insufferable bore with a most limited mentality and a totally materialistic outlook on life.

The professor refuses to permit his daughter to marry Coleman, who is, he informs her, a fraud, a knave, a gambler, and "sporter of fine clothes." He is simply not right for *his* daughter who is intelligent, beautiful, and perfect. Marjory weeps and her tears stir the old man's heart. In her own soft, gentle way, Marjory attempts to explain her lover's qualities to her austere father. He grows impatient, then angry, like the villain in melodramas. Not only will she not marry Coleman, he states, but she must not even call him by his first name. To do so, he claims, is indecorous, even indecent. He launches into a tirade: how could she think of marrying this gambler, this drunkard, this failure? Marjory stands up to her father and quite rightly asks him how he could denigrate a former student of his whom he once admired. Patience eludes Professor Wainwright, particularly when he is cornered. His wishy-washy daughter has won the first round. But now, to save face, the professor is transformed into a "medieval" father. Authority is the answer. He decides on the spot to take his family and some worthy students to Greece. "It has the sanction of antiquity," he reasons. To remove Marjory from Coleman will certainly have the desired effect. With this decision made, Professor Wainwright turns his back on his daughter and goes toward his classroom.

The description of the inclement winter weather adds the right note to the tableau. It emphasizes the darkness and coldness of family relations and the "medieval" aspect of the campus, the defoliated trees like so many skeletons, presaging desolation and sadness.

The image of the "high-walled corridor of one of the castle [college] buildings," strengthens the fortress-like ambience of the college experience, which is, in Crane's opinion, repressive, restrictive, and deleterious to a burgeoning personality. No wonder students feed on extremes, as they do in the next scene, where a group of freshmen and sophomores stream out of a classroom building, fighting with frenzy, gusto, and rage, freshmen and sophomores vying for superiority. Brutality and cruelty are implicit in this altercation.

The combat, waged in the desperation of proudest youth, waxed hot and hotter. The wedge had been instantly smitten into a kind of block of men. It had crumpled into an irregular square and on three sides it was now assailed with remarkable ferocity.

The rushing, screaming, lunging, "lance-attack" that each group makes against the other is, in Crane's view, an indictment of advanced education in America, which he sees as a waste of time, money, and energy. College, then, is a hoax perpetrated on the American public. The "warring hordes" of young men we see here — charging, hurling, punching, pounding out their fury — are a sad but true commentary on some aspects of campus life, particularly during hazing periods. Crane's parody with its overwritten sentences and its flamboyant extremes of mood, ranging from passionate outbursts to controlled acceptance, is stinging.

The Knight to the Rescue

Now a change of scene: the offices of the *New York Eclipse*, the "great" American newspaper. There news items are chosen not for their interest or educational value but rather to feed readers' vicious and sadistic appetites. Coleman is hard at work. Of all the stories brought to his attention, he chooses the birth of "a babe with no arms, born in one of the western counties of Massachussetts . . . In place of upper limbs the child had grown from its chest a pair of finlike hands, mere bits of skin-covered bones. It also had only one eye". This monstrous *thing* will regale readers, become a conversation piece, and delight those who thrive on the wretchedness of others.

Crane's close-up portrait of the *New York Eclipse* is unforgettable. The innuendoes are powerful and far-reaching. Crane mercilessly attacks a crazed, carnivorous public as well as unfeeling newspaper editors with their appetite for horror stories. The *Eclipse* focuses on slander, the monstrous in life, and the freaks of nature. In an article about a shipwreck, the seamen are described as "dead in the rigging of the wreck, a company of grisly and horrible figures, bony-fingered, shrunken and with awful eyes". And for newspaper's photographers and artists are no better; the more gangrenous their shots and drawings, the better it serves to capture attention.

Crane's satire of love of savagery and gore is an attempt to arouse a sense of revulsion for the atrocity stories the *Eclipse* publishes. He achieves the desired effect by juxtaposing harsh, sharp epithets, sequences of alliterations, and a plethora of onomotopeias. Crane also offers his readers an extraordinary picture of the offices of the *Eclipse*: the frantic pace of the staff as they enter and exit from the city editor's office, the interruptions, the calls, and the visitors. The impression of chaos is increased by Crane's use of special verbal ejaculations and rhythmic devices. Journalists intent on selling news items to the city editor express themselves in jarring, screeching, hard tones, their speech fragmented into short clauses, even into words and half

words, which gives the sensation of still more accelera-
tion.

Marjory has asked her father's permission to see
her beloved Coleman once again in order to tell him
that they cannot marry. The professor claims that he
does not want to play the role of the 'obdurate' father;
he has always pictured this kind of person, as featured
in so many novels, "as an exceedingly dense gentleman
with white whiskers who does all the unintelligent
things". Of course, he has become just this kind of
man. As he spits out his hatred for Coleman — the de-
mon, the villain — the scene turns into a melodramatic
comedy. The father gives his daughter permission to
see her beloved once more, then orders her to leave the
room. "Go!" he says, as if gesturing his daughter out of
his life.

No opera of Verdi or Rossini or any other nineteenth-century romantic composer could have captured
this father-daughter altercation in a more melodramatic
manner. The following sequences are also memorable.
Marjory informs her beloved of their tragic situation;
then she announces casually the family's forthcoming
trip to Greece. It will be a lot of "fun" to see new shores,
she explains to Coleman, who reaches out for his beloved's hand, grasps it in "vise-like" manner, and says,
as if he were singing an aria, "Marjory, don't treat me
so! . . . Don't make a fool of me!" At this crucial moment, a student of Professor Wainwright walks in. He
is very rich as well as being favored by Marjory's parents
to become her husband. The lovers have no choice and
bid each other a tearful farewell.

Six weeks pass. Coleman is again featured in his
newspaper office, asking his employer for a much-
needed vacation — to Greece, of course. But how can he
relax there, his employer questions, now that one of
Europe's biggest wars is about to break out? With dignity, Coleman replies that, if there is a war, he will be

on the spot as the *Eclipse's* chief correspondent. The leave is granted. We next see him on shipboard en route to England.

Another romance is in the offing. On board is an actress, Nora Black, whom Coleman knew earlier in his life. She is about to star at the Folly Theatre in London. "A regal creature," with "a sense of mystery that surrounds the lives of the beauties of the stage," Nora Black—modeled after Cora Taylor—uses her wiles to captivate Coleman. "Her voice sank to the liquid siren note of a succubus," writes Crane in an arresting description. Once in London, however, Coleman flees her clutches.

We next see our knight in shining armor at the Hotel d'Angleterre in Athens. Immediately upon his arrival, he inquires about the Wainwright party and is informed by the United States Minister to Greece, the Honorable Thomas M. Gordner, that they have gone to Nikopolis in Epirus, already taken over by the Turks. This particular exchange is based on Crane's own meeting with the United States Minister to Greece, Eben Alexander, to whom he dedicated *Active Service*.

As soon as Coleman hears that the Wainwrights are in grave danger, he assumes the pose of the undaunted knights of old. "He felt on active service," Crane wrote with a tinge of sarcasm and a smattering of mockery, "on active service of the heart," and he felt that he was a strong man ready to conquer any difficulty just as the heroes of old did.

Coleman chooses a dragoman to accompany him on his hazardous trip. Travelling to Patras by train and then continuing on horseback through the danger zone, the journalist notes with precision the bombings and artillery duels. Despite the flying bullets, the astute Coleman leads his guide through the Greek lines. At Arta, he meets other correspondents and also receives cables from the *Eclipse*, which inquire about why he hasn't been heard from. He travels on with his dragoman through heavy rains, suffering the hazards of war. Through the mountains infested with "dead Albanian irregulars" and other sordid sights, they ride on. Suddenly, they realize they are cut off and surrounded by the enemy. Miraculously, they escape and ride off through the dark roads and passes. Without warning, they see forms in the distance and shadows coming toward them. "Halt. Who's there!" Coleman shouts out forcefully. A trembling voice answers, asking the questioner whether he speaks English — an astounding query, since the question was posed in English. Coleman is prepared for the worst, but it is Professor Wainwright and his party from Washurst College. What a fantastic encounter, he thinks, and so does the reader.

Fate has intervened in bringing about a "superb triumph" for Coleman, who will henceforth be looked upon, at least by father and daughter, as their protector, leader, and savior. To think that Coleman, who had never been to Greece before, was able to discover the secret mountain passes and the mysterious forested areas where he, his dragoman, and the Wainwright party could hide, thereby avoiding the Turkish army. But even more incredible is this simultaneous occurrence: Nora shows up on the scene, "smiling and radiant," dressed in a slick riding habit. We learn that she has quit the English stage to follow her beloved to the ends of the earth and she joins the Wainwright caravan, introducing herself as special correspondent for the *New York Daylight*. Coleman, more than distressed, asks her point-blank why she came to Greece. Defiantly she answers, "I came here principally to look for you".

The nascent rivalry between Nora and Marjory kindles new suspense. The rejected suitor, turned knight in shining armor, begins to dislike Nora, fearing she will ruin his relationship with Marjory. But just what is his relationship to this wishy-washy young lady? The conqueror decides to make his position clear, despite the dangers of war and the appearance of a rival woman. Taking Marjory's hand—they are both on horseback—he whispers "swiftly and fiercely in her ear, 'I love you!'" She need not be jealous of Nora, he assures her. The astute Coleman realizes that "in this quick incident they had claimed each other, accepted each other with a far deeper meaning and understanding that could be possible in a mere drawing room. She laid her hand on his arm and with the strength of four men he twisted his horse into the making of furious prancing sidesteps toward the door of the inn." Coleman, a new-born knight seemingly from Sir Walter Scott's *Waverley* series, is ready for the attack whether the enemy be Nora, Mother Wainwright, or the whole Turkish army.

After more harrowing episodes, the Wainwright caravan, Coleman, and Nora return to the Hotel d'Angleterre. Now that the Wainwrights are safe, the downcast Coleman feels he is no longer needed. Marjory will surely reject him to comply with her mother's wishes. Mrs. Wainwright reproaches Coleman for his indecorous conduct: he never should have invited that insidous Nora to join them. What she does not know is that their meeting was fortuitous, not planned.

Marjory, in hysteria, is alone in her room. She refuses to talk to her mother, not wanting to listen to blame or advice. She has established, however, a wonderful rapport with her father—a shock to the reader since only pages earlier the father is depicted as medieval, authoritarian, and narrow-minded. Greece, however, has changed all of this. A pre-Freudian interlude between father and daughter sees the old man kneeling in front of his daughter's bed, listening with rapt attention to her sob-broken speech. She confesses that she has maintained her pride. "Daddy, but I—have—lost—everything—else," she splutters. The father's reaction is a groan. His pain is so keenly felt, his pathos so acute, that he cannot—and this for the first time—articulate his feelings. He is absolutely helpless in this tragedy.

He leaves his daughter's room and coincidentally meets the United States Minister to Greece, who welcomes him back and says about Coleman, "He must be altogether a most remarkable man. When he told me, very quietly, that he was going to try to rescue you, I frankly warned him against any such attempt." With this the professor finally appreciates the real courage displayed by Coleman.

After a brief dinner and an extraordinary conversation with Mrs. Wainwright — extraordinary because of her utter stupidity — the guilt-ridden father returns to his daughter's room. No sooner does she see him then she says: "Daddy, I would like to die. I think — yes — I would like to die." His answer, "Wait!" is a classic of melodrama. With this, he leaves his daughter, goes straight to Coleman, and tells him that he has retracted his objection to their marriage. Before blessing their union, however, he must know just one thing: does Coleman really love Marjory? The answer, as to be expected, is in the affirmative.

The last scene of *Active Service* features Coleman and Marjory resting by the sea. His head touches her knee. Appropriately he exclaims: "I haven't kissed you yet!" — a most remarkable statement for this most unusual spoof of a novel.

The pace of Crane's writing at this period was very rapid in order to meet his high expenses. Although what he had learned in Greece had enriched him both intellectually and psychologically, this wealth of raw material could not possibly be absorbed, evaluated, and distilled fast enough to produce a masterpiece. The satire in *Active Service*, even though occasionally effective and clever, lacks real vigor, strength, and precision. Crane must have sensed this. He wrote the critic, Walter Besant, "I hope that the new book will be good enough to get me to Colorado. It will not be good for much more than that."[1]

Reviewers, respectful of Crane's astounding reputation and admiring of his sincerity, energy, personal
charm, and devotion to various causes, still owed the
truth to their readers. In the London *Times Literary Supplement*, we read that *Active Service* "fails because it tries to
go beyond war, beyond the first palpable shock of battle
and danger. The correspondent is covering a war, but
he is also on active service of the heart; it was a form of
service beyond the scope of Crane's imaginative insight".[2]

7

The O'Ruddy

The O'Ruddy, a suspenseful, picaresque novel about a swashbuckling Irish lad, remained unfinished at the time of Crane's death. He had undertaken the work to pay the staggering debts he and Cora had incurred by their lavish entertainment at Ravensbrook and Brede Manor.

Crane had hoped that Rudyard Kipling would complete *The O'Ruddy*. Although he had deprecated the Englishman's writings in his early days and prided himself on having shed his influence, Crane was, nevertheless, affected by Kipling's spirit and sometimes even his themes, as attested by *The Third Violet*, which is a modification of Kipling's story, *The Light that Failed* (1891). Kipling refused to complete *The O'Ruddy*. His reasons were valid. "My own opinion is, and I hold it very strongly that a man's work is personal to him, and should remain as he made it or left it. I should have been glad to have done him [Crane] a kindness, but this is not a thing that a man feeling as I do can undertake."[1] The task of completing *The O'Ruddy* was left to his friend, Robert Barr, who was thus able to fulfill his promise to the dying Crane.

That Crane could have written a highly dramatic, zestful and exciting picaresque novel at a time when he was in such a weakened and desperate condition is amazing. Certainly, the novel is flawed. Some of the episodes are repetitive and lack the imaginative power of Crane's best work. Still the novel's pace is brisk, and

121

irony and humor are well integrated into the body of the work. The dialogue is replete with Irish epithets and zany phrases that convey instantaneous mood changes and a roguish outlook on life.

The O'Ruddy tells the story of a spirited Irishman born in Glandore. A historical note is introduced to give credibility to the events and characters as well as to enable the reader to understand the many swift moving situations. The protagonist is a soldier of fortune, who sweeps us into his past and then back to his present, divesting events of linear time schemes, just as James Joyce would do a few years later in *Dubliners*:

My ancestors lived in castles which were like churches stuck on end and they drank the best of everything amid the joyous cries of a devoted peasantry. But the good times passed away soon enough and when I had reached the age of eighteen, we had nobody on the land but a few fisherfolks and small farmers, people who were almost law abiding, and my father came to die more from the disappointment than from any other cause. "Tom," he said, "I brought you into existence and God help you safe out of it for you are not the kind of man to ever turn your hand to work and there is only enough money to last a gentleman five more years.

O'Ruddy, our hero, has inherited some money and two swords: a "grand" one that was given to his family by King Louis and "a plain one," which his father told him would surely serve well when the need for it arose. Some important papers also were willed him, but these were returned to the great Earl of Westport living in London.

Three weeks after his father's death, O'Ruddy sets out from Cork, braving storms and gales and finally arriving safely in Bristol, his destination. Teeming with all types of people, the city frightens him at first. Gradually, however, the excitement of the port with its ships coming from countries unknown and its handsomely dressed people as well as its rogues capture his fancy.

O'Ruddy's adventures begin in Bristol: misunderstandings, altercations, and fights. He will not allow himself to be bested by others and speaks out with zest to defend his good name and his family's reputation. To speak the truth, no matter what the consequences, exhilarates him and gives him a sense of his own worth. It also encourages him to fight hard with his fists, kick with his legs, and pierce the heart of his enemies with his sword, which he never hesitates to use.

Although Crane's descriptions are stunning, some critics felt they had fallen into a predictable pattern and that his personifications, color tones, and swift rhythms had become stereotyped. Nevertheless, the energetic brilliance evidenced in Crane's writing is undeniable. The physical world—landscapes, homes, the city, and the countryside—is unforgettably depicted, and the suspenseful events elicit in the reader gloomy or mirthful feelings.

It was a dark and angry morning. The rain swept across my face and the wind flourished my cloak. The road, glistening steel and brown, was no better than an Irish bog for hard riding. . . . I was near journey's end when I came to a portion of the road which dipped down a steep hill. At the foot of this hill was an oak-tree and under this tree was a man masked and mounted and in this man's hand was a levelled pistol. "Stand," he said, "stand!" I knew his meaning.

A highwayman, Jem Bottles by name, stops O'Ruddy on the spot, and the two fire their pistols, neither hurting the other, a typical event in this picaresque adventure tale. The Irishman, confident because of the mysterious power invested in his faithful sword, places it directly "at the highwayman's throat," addressing him in the manner of a Robin Hood: "So, my fine fellow, you rob well. You are the principal knight of the road of all England, I would dare say, by the way in which an empty pistol overcomes you." Crane's highwayman, fearful and meek, is a clever man, bringing his mother into the conversation at the appropriate times as he tells of her sorrow and tears to play on O'Ruddy's sympathy. "Aye . . a true knight of the road with seven ballads written of me in Bristol and three in Bath. I'll betide me for not minding my mother's word and staying at home this day." He once had been an honest sheepstealer; never before had he done anything really terrible — only a little lifting, that's all. O'Ruddy is touched by what he considers Jem Bottles' *true* sorrow. Cheer up, the Irishman tells him; they'll go and see his mother.

In a humorous scene, we meet Jem's hawklike, corrupt, self-seeking mother, who bursts into tears of relief as she sees her son walk in. Joy overcomes her when she learns that the Irishman has decided to take her wayward son with him on his adventures. "I know little of you but, as near as I can see in the light of this one candle, you are an angel. Take my boy! Treat him as you would your own step-son . . . " The two gallop off on their fine steeds — and thus begin a series of harrowing, baffling, blundering adventures, as well as some melodramatic love episodes with Lady Mary, whom O'Ruddy will wed at the end of the novel.

Spontaneity is the hallmark of *The O'Ruddy*. Its variety of scenes are rapidly paced and its multiple characters are endowed with traits such as cowardice, egotism, naiveté, and vanity as well as deeply endearing and lovable qualities. A modern filmmaker might find just the right elements in this amazing novel to present to viewers: moods of merriment and excitement, the reality of social justice and injustice, and various love motifs. An Irish Robin Hood and a modern Tom Jones, O'Ruddy is an immensely appealing character. This fiery and dynamic hero, whose tense adventures in fog-drenched settings are evocative, is whimsical and endearing, a character with whom anyone may readily identify.

Mateo Aleman's picaresque novel, *Guzman de Al-*

farache (1599–1604), Cervantes' *Don Quixote* (1605), Le Sage's *Gil Blas* (1747), and other popular novels all feature the picaroon, or anti-hero, as does *The O'Ruddy*. The picaroon's criminality is frequently seen as mere prankishness. He lives by his wits and is really quite endearing. O'Ruddy acts in keeping with the picaresque tradition, which dramatizes the "rogue" type in all of his engaging immorality and satirizes various social classes. In a sequence of satiric sketches, which serve to knit Crane's loosely connected episodes into a cohesive whole, O'Ruddy outwits those who seek to destroy him.

Crane's picaroon is reminiscent of Tobias Smollett's *Roderick Random* (1748), whose titular hero is in quest of fortune, reveling in prosperity one moment and in destitution the next. Comparisons may also be made with Smollett's *Peregrine Pickle* (1751), whose protagonist is an imaginative young man with a flair for practical jokes. Likewise, O'Ruddy acts frequently in a clownish manner, sometimes behaving like a rascal and sometimes playing the villain. But despite it all, the boyish daredevil Irish lad is essentially good.

The O'Ruddy is far from being a perfect novel; it is overly long and its seemingly endless episodes become monotonous. Still, O'Ruddy's driving, magnetic force equals that of some of Sir Walter Scott's protagonists in his Waverley novels. The dangers and difficulties encountered by Crane's characters are as exciting as those of his English predecessor and their drollery lend a freshness to the novel. Crane proves himself here a masterful story teller and ironist.

The O'Ruddy, though not as carefully constructed as Crane's earlier novels, would be, as noted, a fertile field for the filmmaker. One can visualize an Errol Flynn or a Douglas Fairbanks, Jr. appearing on screen in composites of mobile images and blends of disquieting and romantic episodes. In angle shots, close-ups, fade-outs, and other technical devices, the story takes on the glamor of a resplendent alloy, holding the spectator in its grasp. Scenes designed by Crane to encompass unlimited areas parallel the very goal of cinema. His verbal pictures move, differentiate, and exist with one another in a kind of symbiotic relationship. They are moving pictures, operating in a medium of action. Films rest on a series or accumulation of visual and oral impressions, which electrify the viewer. If the spine-tingling and passionate adventures of Crane's hero were filmed today, they would again delight an audience.

Part III

The Poems

Do not weep, maiden, for war is kind.
Because your lover threw wild hands toward the sky
And the affrighted steed ran on alone,
Do not weep.
War is kind.

> *Harsh, low sound* [handwritten annotation]

    Hoarse, booming drums of the regiment
    Little souls who thirst for fight,
    These men were born to drill and die
    The unexplained glory flies above them
    Great is the battle-god, great, and his kingdom—
    A field where a thousand corpses lie.

Do not weep, babe, for war is kind.
Because your father tumbled in the yellow trenches,
Raged at his breast, gulped and died,
Do not weep.
War is kind.

    Swift, blazing flag of the regiment
    Eagle with crest of red and gold,
    These men were born to drill and die
    Point for them the virtue of slaughter
    Make plain to them the excellence of killing
    And a field where a thousand corpses lie.

Mother whose heart hung humble as a button
On the bright splendid shroud of your son,
Do not weep.
War is kind.

                —Stephen Crane, "War Is Kind"

8

The Black Riders and War Is Kind

Poetry, the medium in which he felt free to express his disjunctive experiences in striking montages, was Crane's shelter. *The Black Riders and Other Lines* (1895) and *War Is Kind* (1899) are distillations of rage and passionate love clothed in tempestuous organic rhythms; each line catches and arrests a fleeting moment. Words recreate sensations of devastation and pain. Crane had a rare ability to compress time through what might be called *freeze framing*. His images are brilliant and concrete.

An anarchic novelist and journalist, Crane rejected the conventional poetic structures of the Harvard-bred group who were his contemporaries: Edwin Arlington Robinson, William Vaughn Moody, Trumbull Stickney, and George Cabot Lodge. Verses welled up from the dream, and Crane's poetic craft was his own. Highbrow philosophical treatises, optimistic cantos praising society's great future, and the sentimental cult of home and family were all rejected by Crane, who offered instead stark feelings evoked through waves of primitive and savage images, filtered of all dross. A terrible sense of isolation and dread saturates line and stanza. From time to time, however, the poet gives us a humanistic vision of a realm of natural goodness hidden behind the static, fatalistic world of his childhood and adolescence.

Crane is not part of the generation of Gertrude Stein, Wallace Stevens, Carl Sandburg, Robert Frost, Edgar Lee Masters, and Vachel Lindsay. Unlike Stein, whose words are chosen for their associations and sound instead of literal definition, and Stevens, whose recondite images and metaphors and intricate stylizations are evocative of French symbolist poems, Crane's poetic vision is visceral and passionate. Like Sandburg, who celebrates America's industry, agriculture, landscape, and history, Crane also melodizes through his bold images and tonal structures, though he focuses on the ravages of war. Like Frost, whose clear and simple bell-like stanzas intone both the beauties of nature and the dark night of the human soul, Crane's ironic, ambiguous, and tenuous verse resounds in the visible world. At times, Crane is as realistic as Masters and as dramatic in his auditory effects as Lindsay. The poetry of Stephen Crane, however, is unique as an expression of bitter outrage and hatred of God.

The Black Riders and *War Is Kind* are reminiscent of both Count of Lautréamont's (1846–1870) *The Songs of Maldoror*, which decried and rebelled against a sadistic diety, and Arthur Rimbaud's (1854–91) *Illuminations* and *A Season in Hell*, which are stunning vilifications of God and society. Like his two predecessors, who each also died at an early age, Crane reached visionary heights in some of his poems, casting off the shackles of mundane aesthetic and philosophical considerations. Straining his faculties to the breaking point, he experienced something similar to what Rimbaud had termed a "rational disorder of the senses."

The Black Riders

The Black Riders brings to mind Emerson's words in "Self-Reliance": "Life only avails, not the having lived. Power ceases in the instant of repose; it resides in the moment of transition from a past to a new state, in the shooting of a gulf, in the darting to an aim."[1] Crane's is *action poetry*, like action painting. It is tense, impulsive, and shocking, shifting its perspectives continuously on an undraped multi-colored inner stage.

The first poem in *The Black Riders* may have been written after a boyhood trip with his mother to Ocean Grove, a Methodist settlement. Seemingly, he had a nightmare shortly thereafter, which depicted a host of black riders rushing up from the sea. Terror filled him, accounting for the disruptive and expansive quality of the verse.

> Black riders came from the sea.
> There was clang and clang of spear and shield,
> And clash and clash of hoof and heel,
> Wild shouts and the wave of hair
> In the rush upon the wind:
> Thus the ride of sin.

Like some of the poems in James Joyce's *Chamber Music* (1907), such as "I hear an army . . . ," and certain cantos of Ezra Pound, Crane opted for hard, clear, and concentrated verse, devoid of syntactical artifices and stilted vocabulary, but replete with orchestrated cadences and visualizations.

A life-force stirs in the stanza quoted and in *The Black Riders*, in general. The urge to burst out of the known into the unknown is evident in Crane's vibrant, cruel, grim, but also beloved landscapes. It can also be seen in his clusters of unorthodox structural units, sequenced epithets, alliterations, onomotopoeias, and clanging sounds, each creating its own startling variety of tones.

The God of organized religion was anathema to Crane. It is against Him and the myth of Creation, the myth of the Flood, and other half-frozen biblical stories that the poet shrieks his anger. Refusing to be a slave of an authoritarian deity, Crane looks into his own cosmos, castigating God for holding on to the rudder while setting the world adrift on its "ridiculous voyages" through spaceless and timeless spheres. "Stupid winds" propel the planet along in pointless turnings and endless turmoils. Pessimism permeates Crane's lines; he feels a deep sense of injustice and betrayal. Yes, God has betrayed humanity.

> God fashioned the ship of the world carefully.
> With the infinite skill of an all-master
> Made He the hull and the sails,
> Held He the rudder
> Ready for adjustment.
> Erect stood He, scanning His work proudly.
> Then — at fateful time — a wrong called,
> And God turned, heeding.
> Lo, the ship, at this opportunity, slipped slyly,
> Making cunning noiseless travel down the ways.
> So that, forever rudderless, it went upon the seas
> Going ridiculous voyages,
> Making quaint progress,
> Turning as with serious purpose
> Before stupid winds.
> And there were many in the sky
> Who laughed at this thing.

A sinister realm comes into view, bringing waves of terror and desperation and isolating the poet in his own bleak tundra.

Haunting shadows inhabit his night, but then, without warning, special luminosities appear: "white arms" kind, warm, and feminine. They will help him through this dark night of the soul and enable him to combat those corrosive forces of "sin" and "damnation."

Should the wide world roll away
Leaving black terror
Limitless night,
Nor God, nor man, nor place to stand
Would be to me essential
If thou and thy white arms were there
And the fall to doom a long way.

To the biblical injunction, "And the sins of the
fathers shall be visited upon the heads of the children,
even unto the third and fourth generation of them that
hate me," Crane retorts:

Well, then, I hate thee, unrighteous picture;
Wicked image, I hate thee;
So, strike with Thy vengeance
The heads of those little men
Who come blindly.
It will be a brave thing.

Rage and bitterness excise the fermenting and putrefy-
ing elements within the universe. The God of wrath,
who beats, storms, and rants, is finally repudiated in a
death-dealing struggle. Gyrating cacophonies and strident, sizzling tones fill the atmosphere with their brutal
reverberations.

The strongest of Crane's anti-God poems begins
with hymnlike majesty, builds up to a frenzy, and finally takes on an apocalyptic dimension as it castigates the
evil God who wreaks havoc upon his creation. Listening with an inner ear and looking with pained eyes, the
poet observes humankind's futile attempts to still a
world rife with contention. In ascending and descend-
ing images, the poet propels his reader into his tormented universe where so many speeding vortices,
each bruising and blurring the other, fighting fruitlessly
and endlessly. Alone, remote, and faint with hunger for

love, the poet stands up fearless to the Almighty God
who tries to beat him down.

> Blustering god,
> Stamping across the sky
> With loud swagger,
> I fear you not.
> No, though from your highest heaven
> You plunge your spear at my heart,
> I fear you not.
> No, not if the blow
> Is as the lightning blasting a tree,
> I fear you not, puffing braggart.

God, the regulating force, dictating the life and death
sequence in the absurd world he brought into existence, reigns with "bloody spears." From the red earth
drenched with human blood, there arise the groans of
men mutilated in body and soul. To this threat of annihilation, the poet responds: "Ah, sooner would I die/
Than see tears in those eyes of my soul."

From his heights, God unleashes bolts of lightning
in an endless "crimson clash of war". Reminiscent of the
cruelties in Oskar Kokoschka's play, *Murderer, Hope of
Women* (1916), Crane's language also verges on the hysterical. It brands and sears flesh and psyche, howling
out its mutinous feelings against warmongers.

> There was crimson clash of war.
> Lands turned black and bare;
> Women wept;
> Babes ran, wondering.
> There came one who understood not these things.
> He said, "Why is this?"
> Whereupon a million strove to answer him.
> There was such intricate clamor of tongues,
> That still the reason was not.

A beatific love, however, redeems the evil forces pervading this God-created world.

> If love loves,
> There is no world
> No world.
> All is lost
> Save thought of love
> And place to dream.
> You love me?

The Black Riders, Crane wrote, was "a more ambitious effort" than *The Red Badge of Courage*. My aim was to comprehend in it the thoughts I have had about life in general, while *The Red Badge* is a mere episode in life, an amplification."[2] When in 1894 he brought his collection of poems to Garland, to whom he had dedicated them, there were no erasure marks and little punctuation on the pages. Garland, marvelling, questioned Crane about his method of composition. Crane pointed to his head and told him: "I've got five or six all in a little row up there. That's the way they come—in little rows, all made up, ready to be put down on paper." Since he wrote with such ease, could he write a poem for him now? Yes, affirmed Crane, seating himself at a table with pencil in hand. Without hesitation, the words poured forth from his "pen like oil."[3] Garland was so impressed that he thought Crane was inhabited by some spirit. Indeed, isn't the poet—the creative being—a vessel for the divine, a *vates*, who speaks what he sees and hears the transcendent language of cosmic spheres?

Crane's publishers were not so impressed as Garland. They wanted him to remove certain poems dealing with his anger against God. Readers would find them objectionable, they said. Crane was annoyed. Were he to omit his wrath against God, he would "cut all the ethical sense out of the book. All the anarchy, perhaps. It is the anarchy which I particularly insist upon." Crane, however, finally acquiesced. Even so, the reviews of *The Black Riders* were mixed. Harry T. Peck in *Bookman* (May, 1895), wrote that Crane's volume of verse was "the most notable contribution to literature to which the present year has given birth." He felt that though there were unrhymed and unrhythmic passages tolling their pessimistic and cynical views, the verses as a whole were fascinating. The poems were praised in the *Atlantic Monthly* for their freshness of vision and potent sensations, though they were "occasionally blasphemous." Howells, however, did not like them at first. A year later he had a change of heart, and, in *Harper's Weekly*, wrote that it was "the best book of the year 1895." Amy Lowell remarked in 1927 that it was a work far before its time: "It is a creed of gall and aloes . . . It is the key to his life. A loathed and vengeful God broods over *The Black Riders*. Crane's soul was heaped with bitterness, and this bitterness he flung back at the theory of life which had betrayed him. His misery and his earnestness made the book, and the supreme irony of all is that it should have been issued as an aesthetic knick-knack and its author hailed as an 'affected ass.'" Other critics found *The Black Riders* brutal and unpalatable; some parodied it. Crane felt scathed by the scurrilous caricatures and declared, "I was the mark for every humorist in the country."[4]

War Is Kind

War Is Kind is also replete with eerie scenes of martyrdom and bone-hard metaphors. Despair, a morbid presence, permeates the world as individuals are forced to endure the agony of war.

Do not weep, maiden, for war is kind.
Because your lover threw wild hands toward the sky
And the affrighted steed ran on alone,
Do not weep.
War is kind.

A litany of solitude, each stanza chants its threnody. The cruelties meted out to human beings haunt the poet as he looks about the great vacant world, with its "dead gray walls" and its "endless silences."

"Where is God?" he questions from his solitary wilderness. An endless desert greets the poet. A sun of blinding radiance pours down its energy. Austerity and asceticism pervade his body, but the *heart* continues beating out its cadences from that spot within which mystics consider *the point of creation*. It is here that the seed germinates, love is kindled, and the poem is born.

Water images abound in *War Is Kind*. The sea, where all is in a state of transition, mediation, and flux, is silent. Pouring forth its overabundant fluid, it drowns and maims, but also enriches life. The sea spreads its "message" in rhythmic assonances and synthesized speech.

No word says the sea, oh, pines
No word says the sea.
Long will your brother be silent to you
Keep his message for the ships
Puny ships, silly ships.

Identified with the maiden, the waters allude to a world of potentialities, to the word, not yet born into the poem.

To the maiden
The sea was blue meadow

Alive with little froth-people
Singing.

Although its action and rhythm are forceful and daring, a sense of stasis, death, and annihilation accompanies these flowing forces.

To the sailor, wrecked,
The sea was dead grey walls
Superlative in vacancy
Upon which nevertheless at fateful time,
Was written
The grim hatred of nature.

Horses burst on the scene, their hoofs and heels
beating down amid repetitive clashings and jarring
onomatopoeia.

Fast rode the knight
With spurs, hot and reeking
Ever waving an eager sword.
"To save my lady!"
Fast rode the knight
And leaped from saddle to war.
Men of steel flickered and gleamed
Like riot of silver sights
And the gold of the knight's good banner
Still waved on a castle wall. . . .
A horse
Blowing, staggering, bloody thing
Forgotten at foot of castle wall.
A horse
Dead at foot of castle wall.

Associated with raw instinct, the horse, as a force of
nature, also represents intense desire and, as such, the
poetic principle. The steed heightens power; it inspires

the writer, allowing him to ride high, lunging ahead, forcing open the barriers that would imprison his incantations. Dedicated to Mars, the god of war, the horse was associated at one time with strife. Also identified with burial rites and chthonian cults, the horse was believed to accompany the dead to their underworld, where the dead were buried and laid to rest. All these associations, particularly the latter, are implicit in the horse imagery in *War Is Kind*.

Like Robinson Jeffers, Crane tends toward a Nietzschean adulation of the forces of nature. Water, wind, earth, and fire are strong and primitive powers, godlike in their beauty. Terrifying and disorienting, they fill the atmosphere with a sense of liberation and elation while annihilating all strictures and constrictions—everything that is anathema to the poet.

> Toward God a mighty hymn
> A song of collisions and cries
> Rumbling wheels, hoof-beats, bells,
> Welcomes, farewells, love-calls, final moans,
> Voices of joy, idiocy, warning, despair,
> The unknown peals of brutes,
> The chanting of flowers
> The screams of cut trees,
> The senseless babble of hens and wise men—
> A cluttered incoherency that says at the stars:
> "O, God, save us!"

Wind cleanses the atmosphere as it inhales and exhales, catalyzing and energizing soul and flesh. Reaching hurricane force, it dislodges and releases the "sin" that had been hermetically sealed in each "fallen" being.

Images are swift and abrasive. Women's voices are heard, sounding their "shrill whistles" in rhythmic reverberations. But now, it is no longer the maiden pure in mind and body whom we see; it is rather the sensual, undulating, snakelike female. Erotic images—reminding one of Charles Baudelaire's dancing woman writhing about like a snake—excite the reader and captivate his senses. The theme of war again engages the poet's attention: "God—the Sky was filled with Armies."

Crane's awesome universe is peopled with blood-soaked images of obscure, evanescent shadows and writhing creatures with dismembered limbs. The "death-demon" looks down upon a chattering, fearful, and agonized humanity.

"Intrigue," Crane's group of love poems, are neither interesting nor innovative. They deal mostly with his love for Lily Brandon Munroe, whom Crane visited before returning to England.

> Thou art my love
> And thou art the peace of sundown
> When the blue shadows soothe
> And the grasses and the leaves sleep
> To the song of the little brooks
> Woe is me.

Although they evoke distress and passion, they lack vigor and the spectacular passion that is Crane's hallmark.

Crane, the word virtuoso, bursts into life in *The Black Riders* and *War Is Kind*—poems in which emotions boil and overflow in brilliant metaphors. As seer, Crane fuels his furnacelike eye and hurls forth his sparkling verbal images. Because he did not work on his poems—they catapulted from his head in pre-fashioned lines—critics found their disjointed, aggressive images and savage mixed metaphors barbaric. The poems' devouring colors, burning and bruising syntax, flaming anger against God, moroseness and bitterness, assaults against organized religion, and anarchic technique were more than people at that time could accept.

Crane did have his defenders and admirers. Edward Garnett thought the poems in *The Black Riders* "as sharp in their naked questioning as sword blades."[5] Harry Thurston Peck wrote, in the *Bookman*, that "Mr. Crane is a true poet whose verse, long after the eccentricity of form has worn off, fascinates us and forbids us to lay the volume down." Carl Sandburg, in his poem "Letter to Dead Imagists" (1916), looked upon Crane's irregular metrics and formless verse as validation of his poetic technique. Ezra Pound considered Crane a precursor of Imagism.[6] Whatever the consensus, "Do not weep, maiden, for war is kind" is one of the most extraordinary war poems of all time.

Part IV

The Tales

His art does not include the necessity for complex arrangements; his sure instinct tells him never to quit the passing moment of life, to hold fast by simple situations, to reproduce the episodic, fragmentary nature of life in such artistic sequence that it stands in place of the architectural masses and co-ordinated structure of the great artists.

— Edward Garnett, "Mr. Stephen Crane: An Appreciation"

9

Tales of Adventure

The thirteen short stories in *Tales of Adventure* deal with three periods in Crane's life: his Asbury Park boyhood, his trip to the West and to Mexico in 1895, and his Cuban venture in 1897.

In his short stories, Crane adheres to Poe's dictum: the tale should form a "totality. . . . there should be no word written, of which the tendency, direct or indirect, is not to the one pre-established design."[1] Like a poem, each tale forms a complete unit, every portion contributing to its final impact and effect upon the reader. Each tale is a self-contained drama. Some have a sting to them; others have an epigrammatic quality that intensifies their momentum and shattering climax. Excitement is generated by controlled, barely sensed actions, which may be nothing more than a minor occurrence, such as a blizzard. Crane's tales aim at realism. They deal with the conflict between illusion and reality or the inner and outer worlds. Neither romantic nor charming, as are Washington Irving's *The Sketch Books*, Crane's stories show detachment, coldness, and a remote quality, lending a mythical touch to such tales as "The Bride Comes to Yellow Sky" or "The Open Boat." A feeling for nature and for natural man is molded directly into his colorful landscapes and precise descriptions of people and things. The earthiness of his terse, colloquial dialogue is alternately humorous, sardonic, and searing. The stories' musicality also lends them a poetic and incantatory quality.

Crane did not probe his characters' souls as Hawthorne did. Instead he silhouetted them in the light of specific situations or through character traits, giving brief insights here and there. Like Twain, he injected humor into his stories — not *Huckleberry Finn*'s light-hearted banter, but rather satire wedded to bold similes. Unlike Twain, he never romanticized his protagonists nor alluded to nostalgic moments. Crane banished sentimentality and gushy romance, opting for realistic optical images, which under scrutiny reveal the truth of a situation. In this art form, Crane is on a par with masters such as Maupassant, Flaubert, Chekhov, Tolstoy, Gogol, Melville, Hawthorne, James, and Conrad. He knew how to use form, color, and drama to heighten the desired effects. Crane was a superb verbal photographer. His close-up and distant shots, posessed of some indefinable magical powers, remain indelibly fixed in the mind's eye.

"The Pace of Youth" (1895) is situated in the seaside resort of Asbury Park, New Jersey, where the twelve-year old Crane lived with his widowed mother. It focuses on a single image of intense appeal to a child: a glittering and exciting merry-go-round, which dominates not only the events but the characters as well. Stimson is the owner of the "Mammoth Merry-Go Round," with its "whirling circle of ornamental lions, giraffes, camels, ponies, goats, resplendent with varnish and metal that caught swift reflections from windows high above them." The fabulous carousel elicits excitement and ebullience from the children, who cling to the animals on which they ride. Amid all of this joy stalks Stimson, who has learned of his daughter Lizzie's elopement with Frank, his impresario. Despite his wife's pleading, he takes his revolver and runs "hatless" to hail a hack. Once inside, he orders the driver to gallop through the streets and catch up with the buggy that

Lizzie and her lover had taken moments earlier. Excitement is intensified as the two vehicles race each other. But when Stimson realizes his hack is falling behind, his hopes of stopping his daughter are dashed. "His whole expedition was the tottering of an old man upon the trail of birds," Crane explains. Age has intervened; the generation gap has made inroads in his relationship with his daughter. He represents a dying past; she, the joyous future. Stimson gives up the race. It is no use. As he makes "a gesture of acquiescence, rage, despair" he suddenly becomes aware of the fact that he forgot his hat. This detail is of monumental importance since it makes him realize that he is no longer in the running.

"One Dash—Horses" (1896) was the first of a group of tales Crane wrote about his trip to the West and Mexico. For some years he had dreamt of seeing those open spaces and endless skies. He was fascinated by the myth of this land of promise and excitement with its very different codes, customs, and characters.[2]

"One Dash—Horses" is based on a real incident in which Crane and his guide, riding into Mexican back country, spent the evening in a local adobe tavern. When Crane saw a drunken bandit, Ramon Colorado, eyeing him, obviously thinking Crane was a "rich" American, he reached for his revolver and stared unflinchingly at the bandit. Ramon Colorado, stunned by the courage of this foreigner, seems then to have changed his mind. The arrival on the scene of girls and musicians draws the bandit's attention away from Crane and his guide, permitting them to slip out of the tavern, mount their horses, and ride away. Soon, however, they notice they are being pursued by the bandit and his cohorts. The terror in their hearts encourages them to gallop on until they meet a troop of rural militia.

Crane does not emphasize the men in his tale; instead he focuses on and humanizes the horses. For example, when the narrator, fearing for his life, drives his steed to incredible speed he looks at the animal with deep confidence, as if it also knew the danger at stake: "The little animal, unurged and quite tranquil, moving his ears this way and that way with an air of interest in the scenery, was nevertheless bounding into the eye of the breaking day with the speed of a frightened antelope." Having reached safety, the narrator again stares at his little horse and becomes aware of his deep love for the animal.

The protagonist's terror is depicted as a race against time. The speed of hoofbeats as bits and pieces of landscape flash by, the rhythmic noise of the dashing horses, the sweat and breathlessness generated by the tremendous effort being expended symbolize the chaos of the unresolved situation. In the tavern scene, for example, fear is built up by foreboding reds and lambent hues: "the deep silence of the pale rays of the moon" as opposed to "the red spears of the fire," shedding their tones in a room "slowly flooded to its middle with a rectangle of silver light." Through economy of words Crane achieves a work of powerful impact.

"The Wise Men" (1896) is virtually plotless and does not have the sweep or scope of the earlier tales. It is, however, more complicated psychologically.

Two Kids enter the Cafe Colorado: its "front of white and gold, in which is set larger plate-glass windows than are commonly to be found. Two little wings of willow flip-flapping incessantly serve as doors." One of the Kids is from New York and the other from San Francisco; they resemble each other and are always together, "youths of subtle mind. . . . wicked according to report." A race is to be held at midnight between Pop, the Cafe's aging manager, and a young man, Freddie. Tension mounts. For whom will the Kids bet? They take their time and sit down at a table to order a salad. "They were always ordering salads. This was because one Kid had a wild passion for salads, and the other didn't care much." The juxtaposition of the seemingly inconsequential salad-eating episode with the seriousness of the race invites laughter and thereby disrupts the story's focus and its strained atmosphere. The Kids bet on Pop, who has given them his assurance that he "can run like a rabbit." The old man wins. The Kids, in contrast to the habitues who bet on youth, are the "wise men" of the tale. The stark simplicity of the dialogue and the Kids' singleness of purpose capture an entire sequence of events in this terse and witty tale.

"The Five White Mice" (1896) is a wry story that again features two gun-slinging, venturesome, jocular youths, the San Francisco and New York Kids. After failing with dice, the gambler's motto seems as effective a credo as anything else:

> Oh, five white mice of chance,
> Shirts of wool and corduroy pants,
> Gold and wine, women and sin,
> All for you if you let me come in —
> Into the house of chance.

After rolling up more and more aces, the New York Kid finds himself and his two drunken companions, the San Francisco Kid and Benson, facing some Mexican desperados on a street, "as dark as a whale's throat at deep sea." The sober Kid is terrified; he remembers what easterners had said about western lawlessness, about the cruelty of cowboys and desperadoes. He sees himself dead and his family grieving for him. He waits, motionless, as he observes his enemies. He is terrified at the thought that he might not be able to draw his gun quickly enough. What if he drops it at the crucial moment or it gets entangled in his coat tails? "The sober Kid saw this [Mexican] face as if it were alone in space — a yellow mask smiling in eager cruelty, in satisfaction, and above all it was lit with sinister decision." The Kid suddenly decides to step forward. He grips his revolver. Crane increases the suspense by taking a moment out to caricature the entire incident, inviting the reader into the Kid's imaginary world. "He recalled that upon its black handle was stamped a hunting scene in which a sportsman in fine leggings and a peaked cap was taking aim at a stag less than one eighth of an inch away." The contrast between the gravity of the Kid's present situation and the romantic visions carved on the holster of his revolver encourages wry laughter along with feelings of fright at the thought of the dangers at stake. "At the supreme moment the revolver came forth as if it were greased and it arose like a feather. This somnolent machine, after months of repose, was finally looking at the breasts of men." The reader learns, in a form of interior monologue, why the Kid was filled with rage as he took aim. The Mexicans "slunk back, their eyes burning wistfully," never giving him a chance to prove his courage. "The whole thing had been an absurd imposition." They all leave. "Nothing had happened". Nothing, yet everything is compressed into that one traumatic incident: fear, self-pity, courage, and will power.

"A Man and Some Others" (1897) also deals with the trauma of sustained terror and the serenity that follows the acceptance of one's mortality. A sheepherder, Bill, decides to fight the murderers stalking him. Feelings of anxiety and alienation build as Crane focuses his camera's eye on stark background images: "Dark mesquit spread from horizon to horizon. There was no house or horseman from which a mind could evolve a city or a crowd. The world was declared to be a desert and unpeopled." Crane now fills the reader in on Bill's past, giving the present situation a sense of perspective. Bill was once the owner of a rich mine in Wyoming, but lost the mine playing poker. He then became a cowboy, gambled again, and once again found himself destitute. He then worked as a bouncer, a killer, and, finally, a sheepherder in Texas. The story now pursues its course in the present. A Stranger approaches Bill, who warns him to leave because killing is in the offing. Minutes later, some Mexicans charge Bill. The Stranger screams. "As the guns roared, Bill uttered a loud grunt, and for a moment leaned panting on his elbow, while his arm shook like a twig. Then he upreared like a great and bloody spirit of vengeance, his face lighted with the blaze of his last passion." Bill is dead.

A sense of compassion, greater, perhaps, than in Crane's previous stories, prevails in "A Man and Some Others." Bill's past and his laconic statements to the Stranger let the reader understand the dignity of a man who once was a killer and the ease with which life may be ended. At the end of the tale, the Stranger looks at the "body contorted, with one arm stiff in the air" that lies in his path. "Slowly and warily he moved around it, and in a moment the bushes, nodding and whispering, their leaf-faces turned toward the scene behind him, swung and swung again into stillness and the peace of the wilderness."

"The Open Boat" (1898), one of America's finest short stories, describes the adventure that satisfied Crane perhaps most fully. He said once that he wanted to go "to some quarter of the world where mail is uncertain." He did just that when he accepted Bacheller's assignment in November, 1896 to cover the Cuban Revolution. Thick fog enshrouded the St. Johns River as the Commodore set sail from Jacksonville with Crane aboard. Although Captain Edward Murphy had taken the precaution of hiring a local pilot to help the vessel out of the harbor, it struck a sand bar. The following morning, the Commodore was towed free, but Murphy neglected to review the damage done the ship, which continued on into deeper waters. By the time the leak was discovered, there was no hope of saving the ship. Although the Captain tried to steer it back to the harbor, the pumps and engines gave out and it foundered. Passengers and crew were ordered into the lifeboats. Crane's conduct during this harrowing ordeal was superb: he soothed frightened men, helped bail out water, and acted like a born sailor. After the crew was in the lifeboats, Crane, the Captain, the cook and the oiler climbed into a ten-foot-long dinghy.

Although the boat managed to stay afloat on the high seas, Crane's harrowing experience was far from over. The mate's lifeboat capsized and the men on it drowned. Crane was deeply moved by the courage of the sailors who drowned: no shrieks, no groans, only silence.[3]

The remaining lifeboats reached land the following day. The dinghy, however, could not get ashore because of the rough surf and so remained out at sea. No one on shore could see or hear the men in the dinghy. The captain fired his pistol but to no avail, and the men were forced to spend another night in the dinghy, rowing frantically to prevent being swallowed up by the rough seas. They then decided to row to Daytona Beach and try to make it through the breakers there. But the boat overturned, and they had to swim. A man on the beach saw what happened and ran for help. All but the oiler were saved.

"None of them knew the color of the sky," is perhaps one of the most celebrated opening lines of any short story. The opening line conveys the fierce struggle between finite man and the infinitude that engulfs him — as in Melville's *Moby-Dick*. The sea for Crane, as it is for Melville, is "the image of the ungraspable phantom of life."[4]

The men's agony at not knowing their fate is underscored by the power of those surging waters — waves that could sweep the men under at any moment. The horizon narrowed and widened, and dipped and rose, at all times its edge was jagged with waves that seemed thrust up in points like rocks."

Man, like the helpless survivors in the boat, is thrust here and there and floats about in utter helplessness. No matter how hard people try to fix and direct themselves, they are castaways. Salvation — if there is one — lies in the bonds between men that assuage their implacable solitude.

The craft pranced and reared, and plunged like an animal. As each wave came, and she rose for it, she seemed like a horse making at a fence outrageously high. The manner of her scramble over these walls of water is a mystic thing, and moreover, at the top of them were ordinarily these problems in white water, the foam racing down from the summit of each wave, requiring a new leap, and a leap from the air.

Crane's use of changing rhythms throughout the tale points up the terror of the dinghy's passengers and exemplifies the utter senselessness of existence itself.

Crane suggests that if an observer were to look upon the events objectively, viewing them "from a balcony, the whole thing would doubtless have been weirdly picturesque. But the men in the boat had no time to see it, and even if they had had leisure, there were other things to occupy their minds". Values of virtue, bravery, integrity were once of importance, but now are meaningless in a godless universe where nature observes impassively human despair and frustration. Yet, the harrowing sea journey creates a new morality, which gives fresh meaning to life: "the brotherhood of men . . . was established on the seas. No one said that it was so. No one mentioned it. But it dwelt in the boat, and each man felt it warm him". Comfort and feelings of well-being emerge as each helps the other assuage his growing terror.

In the midst of fear and harrowing terror, there is also irony and humor:

If I am going to be drowned—if I am going to be drowned—if I am going to be drowned, why, in the name of the seven mad gods who rule the sea, was I allowed to come thus far and contemplate sand and trees? Was I brought here merely to have my nose dragged away as I was about to nibble the sacred cheese of life? It is preposterous. If this old ninny-woman, Fate, cannot do better than this, she should be deprived of the management of men's fortunes. She is an old hen who knows not her intention. If she has decided to drown me, why did she not do it in the beginning and save me all this trouble. The whole affair is absurd. . . . But, no, she cannot mean to drown me. Not after all this work.

A mystical relationship exists between the men in the dinghy—and the sea and heavens. Crane feels compelled to point out man's smallness, to set him back into nature and reduce him to size.

Conversations between the oiler and the cook, seemingly trivial, since they revolve around food—"What kind of pie do you like best?"—serve in reality to point out the absurdity of humankind's preoccupations. They also act as a way of dispelling progressive terror. As for the captain, he is ridiculed; the men laugh at him, again distracting themselves from their great fear of death.

The sight of a shark heightens the men's dreadful tension. Crane does not mention the shark by name, but the reader can almost hear the shark's fin cut the water's surface and see its phosphorescent gleaming body. Like the survivors of "Raft of the Medusa," whose harrowing episode is famous in French maritime history, the men in the dinghy do not know there is a lifesaving station twenty miles away.

When the ordeal is over, the men, safely on land, look back at the water: "white waves paced to and fro in the moonlight, and the wind brought the sound of the great sea's voice to the men on shore, and they felt that they could then be interpreters." The narrator's voice withdraws, as it were, from the chaotic drama, introducing a sense of spatial and temporal distance. Comfortable on land, the narrator can indulge in the luxury of waxing poetic and thus transform subjective emotions into a work of art.

Its poetry and rhythmic schemes make "The Open Boat" the match of Melville's "White Jacket" and the best of Jack London and Joseph Conrad. This tale's unusually punctuated sentences of contrasting length simulate the heart beat of man under extreme stress, producing an incantatory quality. Crane's sensual images of man struggling against the sea remain vivid long after the reading of "The Open Boat." The salt spray and deafening roar of the waves pounding against the dinghy can almost be tasted and heard.

"Flanagan and His Short Filibustering Adventure" (1898) also focuses on the sea. Written under intense pressure, the story is entertaining, but not comparable to "The Open Boat" in either technique or subject matter.

"The Bride Comes to Yellow Sky" (1898), however, is another masterpiece of restraint, concision, and heart-stirring drama. The action takes place mostly in the mind of Sheriff Jack Potter, who goes off to San Antonio to bring back his bride to Yellow Sky. Disquietude and guilt seem to mark his every thought and gesture during the long train trip home with his new wife. The "heinous crime" that torments Sheriff Potter is that he has not informed his friends—the citizens of Yellow Sky—about his forthcoming marriage. The personality of the groom—in contrast with the usual image of the Western sheriff who with gun and badge imposes order on a lawless society—is revealed as he looks at his bride tenderly and shyly shows her "the dazzling fittings of the coach." Although trying to impress her, the sheriff remains modest and humble. He then slips into town via the back entrance in order to keep out of sight.

The couple has almost reached their home when a drunken outlaw, Scratch Wilson, approaches them and pulls out his gun. He intends to settle his affairs by fighting Potter. "I ain't got a gun on me, Scratchy," answers the Sheriff. Scratchy doesn't believe him. How could a sheriff be unarmed? "If you ain't got a gun, why ain't you got a gun? Been to Sunday-school?" When Potter tells him he has just been married, Scratch Wilson is stunned—he "was like a creature allowed a glimpse of another world. He moved a pace backward, and his arm with the revolver dropped to his side."

Sheriff Potter broke the frontier code in two respects: by his marriage, and being gunless. His image tarnished, he is no longer a role model. Scratch Wilson can not conceive of living in a town with a married sheriff. As for Potter's not carrying a gun: "There ain't a man in Texas ever seen you without no gun." Like the Sheriff, whose train trip was so filled with anxiety, Scratch is also caught in a maze. This new situation spells trepidation. A single incident serves to point up the meaning of dread, not the dread encountered in "The Open Boat," but the fear of change and apprehension that comes with the shattering of illusions and preconceived notions. With humor and irony, Crane demolishes the images of the brash, aggressive, loud-mouth sheriff and the blood-thirsty outlaw and creates instead the two unforgettable characters of "The Bride Comes to Yellow Sky."

"Death and the Child" (1898) is more discursive and less densely wrought. It concerns a foreign correspondent, Peza, who is sent to Greece. While there he discovers that his Greek heritage makes him become emotionally involved with the people he was sent to write about. He also comes to learn, as do many of Crane's protagonists including Henry Fleming in *The Red Badge of Courage*, that his preconceived ideas of war do not fit reality.

The opening of "Death and the Child" gives the reader a frightening image of peasants streaming down a mountain trail as they flee the enemy.

The cattle and the huge round bundles seemed to suffice to the minds of the crowd if there were now two in each case where there had been three. This brown stream, poured on with a constant wastage of goods and beasts. . . . A colt, suddenly frightened, made a stumbling charge up the hillside.

It seems that every living thing is fleeing "with every tie severed that binds us to the soil. . . ." Stunned by the suffering and cruelties of war, Peza keeps repeating: "I had no dream — I had no dream that it would be like this! This is too cruel! Too cruel!" He decides immediately to join forces with the Greeks and fight against the Turks. The officer in charge smiles at the naive correspondent, who cringes at the sight of the dying men around him and the noise of bullets detonating in the distance. "It was sounding in regular measures like the beating of a colossal clock — a clock that was counting the seconds in the lives of the stars, and men had time to die between the ticks." The lieutenant points in the direction of the conflagration. "Well, there!" he said. "If you wish for war you now have an opportunity magnificent." Peza looks at this "great carnival of woe," then, to the "river of fleeing villagers." There were no "pageants of carnage" in his childhood dreams of fighting enemies. He realizes now that "this theatre for slaughter, built by the inscrutable needs of the earth, was an enormous affair, and he reflected that the accidental destruction of an individual, Peza by name, would perhaps be nothing at all".

Peza walks on and sees some soldiers in the trenches. Nearby, he sees a small child playing in front of the little cobbled hut from which his parents fled. A cow lives in it now. The child seems to be oblivious to terror. He continues running "to and fro, fumbling with sticks and making great machinations with pebbles." The child ceases to play and begins to weep. He is hungry and calls for his mother. The rattle of some loose stones distracts him from his sorrow. He walks over to the spot where the noises are coming from and sees a "heaving form" covered with dust. "Are you a man?" the child asks. Deeply touched by the scene, Peza cannot answer.

Peza's psychology fascinates Crane. Peza dreams of helping an imperilled people, believing that a Greek victory would preserve the fatherland. He flees, however, at a crucial moment of the war, his romantic illusions shattered by the sound of the exploding shells and the sight of destruction. Peza comes to understand his foibles and his fears by projecting them on the child who, engrossed in his own little world, expresses his physical distress through tears. For Peza, the child is *everyman* at the beginning and end of the ordeal that is life. Preoccupied by his own imaginary wars, the child is unaware of reality. Neither naive nor innocent, he is potential man.

"Death and the Child" is based in part on Crane's own experience as a war correspondent in Greece. The dispatches he wrote there captured the flavor and excitement as well as the turmoil and terror of war. These are the elements that H. G. Wells saw as "a new ingredient" in Crane's short story—"an ingredient imposed on Crane's natural genius from without—a concession to the demands of a criticism it had been wiser, if less modest in him to disregard. . . . "[5] Journalism, Wells concluded, had imposed its necessities upon Crane's creative élan. His work had to sell and therefore be slick and contrived. No longer could he follow his own bent.

"The Blue Hotel" (1898), which takes place at Fort Romper, Nebraska, is another of Crane's finest tales. It has many facets. Each character plays a role in keeping with his personality. Although the narrator apprehends only some of the truths implicit in the tale, the reader, through the metaphor of the blue hotel, is able to grasp the entire picture.

The Palace Hotel in Nebraska is painted blue, a fact of utmost importance: "a light blue, a shade that is on the legs of a kind of heron, causing the bird to declare its position against any background". This premonitory image, offered the reader at the very outset of the tale, implies metaphorically the fixity and intractability of the protagonist's view of people.

A Swede enters the Blue Hotel. Like the heron in the opening image, he is anchored to his unalterable preconceptions. He is certain that the people frequenting the Blue Hotel are lawless and cruel and that he may even be killed here. He masks his terror by adopting a swaggering gait and behaving in an arrogant manner. Like several other of Crane's characters, the Swede is an easterner prejudiced against the Wild West by dime novels and not by real life. Scully, the proprietor of the hotel, reveals himself to be just the opposite of the Swede's notion of the gun-happy Westerner; in fact, he looks "curiously like an old priest." He offers the Swede warmth, hospitality, and a drink in a show of friendliness, but to no avail. The Swede continues to act aggressively and defiantly. He even insults the proprietor and the habitués. "A guest under my roof has sacred privileges," Scully says. But the friendliness Scully offers the Swede is rejected. The Swede is convinced that the Blue Hotel, which looks more like a church with its icons and stained glass windows, spells violence and death.

Scully persists; he offers the Swede a fine meal and encourages him to join a group of friendly card players. The Swede then accuses the host's son, Johnny, of cheating, and a fight breaks out. Of course, Johnny is no match for the Swede. He is knocked to the ground almost immediately and the Swede would have continued hitting him had the others not intervened.

The Swede, convinced that he is in *real* danger, leaves the Blue Hotel in a blizzard to search for a safe place. "In front of it [another bar] an indomitable red light was burning, and the snow-flakes were made blood-color as they flew through the circumscribed territory of the lamp's shining." Another premonitory image: the red light presages blood and death. The Swede enters the "sanded expanse before him" and pours himself a whiskey. He then begins boasting of having "thumped the soul out of a man down here at Scully's hotel". Those present "encased themselves in reserve" and when the Swede invites the guests — a gambler, businessmen, a district attorney, and others — to drink with him, they refuse with "quiet dignity." Enraged by their rejection, the Swede virtually explodes. Putting his hand on the shoulder of the gambler, he invites him once again to drink with him and is once again refused. "What? You won't drink with me, you little dude! I'll make you!" the Swede roars, holding the gambler by the throat and dragging him from his chair.

There was a great tumult, and then was seen a long blade in the hand of the gambler. It shot forward, and a human body, this citadel of virtue, wisdom, power, was pierced as easily as if it had been a melon. The Swede fell with a cry of supreme astonishment.

The story does not end with this. Crane must add his dash of irony. The gambler is given three years in prison for murder. As for Johnny of the Blue Hotel, he *had* cheated, the reader learns, but because "the game was only for fun." The guest who actually saw the sleight of hand had said nothing. Everyone, then, is guilty of the Swede's murder, Crane suggests — the criminal who did the stabbing as well as the collective who did nothing to prevent it.

Fear, masked by arrogance, and the impossibility of modifying role models are the themes of "The Blue Hotel." The fierce, graphic descriptions of the howling blizzard reproduce the nerve-shattering momentum built up within the hotel. The tale revolves around the Swede, who harangues and assaults the other guests, projecting his own inadequacies upon them. Because he wants to give the impression of being strong and virile, he has built up a paranoic system of defenses against presumed enemies. Scully, the spiritual leader of the hotel group, prevents an outbreak of violence as long as it is humanly possible. The Swede's heavy drinking, begun in the Blue Hotel, continues in the saloon. He feels manic elation over his victory in his fight with Johnny. The blinding snowstorm symbolizes the Swede's lack of vision, his inability to see into himself and, therefore, into others. He is unable to assimilate the kindness he was shown at the Blue Hotel; nor can he interpret the harsh atmosphere of the saloon. Like the heron of the opening image, he stands fixed in his ideas, oblivious to his surroundings, and it is his rigidity and blindness that cause his death.

Like "The Open Boat," "The Blue Hotel" deals with the theme of brotherhood as well as that of hostility. The Swede is given shelter from the storm, and is invited into a community of friendly people. But because they failed to understand the meaning behind the Swede's hostile behavior, the other characters are as blind and set in their ways as the Swede. As Crane suggested, "The Blue Hotel" is "a whirling, fire-smitten, ice-locked, disease-stricken space-lost bulb"—a microcosm of society and the world.

Fascinated by the dichotomies of eastern and western landscapes, of wild and churning seas, Crane, like Melville, Poe, and Conrad, uses his painter's eye to reveal strikingly vast spaces and war-torn areas. His verbal canvases, marked in blues, whites, reds, ochres, browns and blacks, portray scrubby ranges, low hills, blinding snows, and ferocious seas. He uses the detail to reveal the whole; he scrutinizes the isolated incident to explain the larger drama. He reveals a personality type in a swift and often elliptical manner, a situation in stonelike, language divested of all extraneous elements.

10

Tales of War

Crane's war tales include: *The Little Regiment* (1896), which dealt with Civil War episodes, written prior to Crane's having witnessed any real action in a war; "An Episode of War," completed after he had seen the battle of Velestino, and *Wounds in the Rain* (1900), which focused on episodes of the Cuban war; and *Spitzbergen Tales* (1900), four stories focusing on a fictional Spitzbergen army.

The Little Regiment

The six tales comprising *The Little Regiment* are contrived and lack vigor and originality. They are the product of a writer at odds with himself, whose intentions are noble, but whose final work often founders in banalities. Crane realized the limitations of these tales better than anyone else when he wrote: "I have invented the sum of my invention with regard to war and this story keeps me in internal despair."[1] Despite the book's many failings, however, some critics lauded Crane's fine achievement: "Mr. Crane's war episodes are like clippings out of the great book of war itself, realistic in the best sense, and in *The Little Regiment* he fully sustains the surprising power he first displayed in *The Red Badge of Courage*." His artistic acumen also was praised: "Great dashes of crimson and blobs of blue break occasionally through the dim and mystic clouds of grey mist, and the whole demoniacal howling of the battle quivers in our brain for hours . . . " His use of adjectives is striking, comparable to Walt Whitman's unforgettable visualizations in *Memoranda During War*; his panoramic delineations of battle scenes are reminiscent of Tolstoy's *War and Peace*; as for his daring portrayals of heroism and his depictions of man's bestiality, these too are arresting; and his humor adds a bit of comic relief to what might have remained utterly morbid. It is to be noted that President McKinley, a soldier himself, spoke with high regard of *The Little Regiment*. With tongue in cheek, Crane responded: "He would know if the stuff was real or not, even if he can't write good English."[2]

The first tale, "The Little Regiment," presents a fascinating psychological situation. Two brothers, Dan and Billie, love each other deeply, but are incapable of expressing their feelings except by disparaging one another. So overt is their seeming antagonism that "when entertaining quarrels were lacking, their companions often contrived situations calculated to bring forth display of this fraternal dislike."

To heighten the sense of mystery surrounding the brothers' relationship, Crane has to recourse to canvases of mists, each one curtaining or veiling actuality. "In one mystic changing of the fog, as if the fingers of spirits were drawing aside these draperies, a small group of the grey skirmishers, silent, statuesque" are revealed. Similarly, Crane's auditory tonalities — thunderings of musketry and shrill cries — add to the grandiose drama of the tale.

The fog rarely lifts for the brothers: each lives blanketed in his own repressed world, ashamed of revealing his true feelings to the other for fear of being accused of weakness. Strong and hardworking, Dan and Billie are devoted to their regiment, experiencing "the fierce elation" brought on by the terrors of war.

Only once do the brothers reveal themselves plain. After Billie has been reported dead, Dan sees a man coming down the street whose head is bandaged. "Dan started. His skin of bronze flushed to his temples. He seemed about to leap from the ground, but then suddenly he sank back, and resumed his impassive gazing." The brothers are together again, and silence reigns. Billie finally says, "Hello, Dan." And his brother answers, "Hello, Billie". The restraint and simplicity of Crane's conclusion is stunning.

The second tale, "Three Miraculous Soldiers," is more conventional. It deals with a young girl who, having read about heroines when she was at boarding school in Pennsylvania, is inspired to save the lives of three southern soldiers by hiding them inside a barn in a horse's feed box.

"A Mystery of Heroism: A Detail of an American Battle" is a significant tale because the action for the most part takes place in the mind of a soldier as he meditates on the meaning of courage and violence. What does bravery involve? What are the effects of a gratuitous act? What is fate?

Crane uses a cinematographic technique in "A Mystery of Heroism: A Detail of an American Battle." He depicts an army in the thick of combat and then focuses on Fred Collins of Company A as he complains of thirst. Larger frames are then churned out: a horse being killed, a shelled farmhouse, gunners fighting, wounded soldiers, two privates arguing about political matters. As enemy fire accelerates, Collins's clamoring for water becomes more vociferous. His fellow soldiers laugh at him and then encourage him to go through enemy fire to get water. When Collins receives permission to do so, no one understands why he wants to take the chance of being killed when no one, not even he, strangely enough, is *really* thirsty. Is it a question of pride? Is it a gratuitous act? As Collins begins his dangerous trek, the changing war images measure the barometer of his emotions. Because Collins knows no fear, he is convinced that he is a hero. Crane, however, mocks the very concept of heroism: "He was not a hero. Heroes had no shame in their lives, and, as for him, he remembered borrowing fifteen dollars from a friend and promising to pay it back the next day, and then avoiding that friend for ten months." Collins is not a hero after all. As Collins pursues his lonely walk, he is suddenly panic-stricken, having become aware of strengths and his weaknesses. He sees a wounded officer, and despite the man's cries for water, walks on, so fearful is he for his own life. Moments later, gripped with guilt or compassion or a delayed sense of duty—and herein lies *the mystery*—Collins returns to the dying man and gives him some water, convinced that to help someone in need is an indication of great courage. When Collins finally returns to his company, two officers begin playing with the filled bucket and, ironically, the water spills out onto the earth.

Crane's use of the word *mystery* in the title implies that certain acts during a time of crisis must remain unexplained. What were Collins's motives for getting the water? Was it worth risking his life to do so? Why did he decide to return to give the dying soldier some water? And why, in the end, was his travail for nought? The human personality is as unfathomable and baffling as the savagery—and, for Crane, the beauty—of war. What makes "A Mystery of Heroism" so effective is the way in which Crane mounts his close ups and distant shots. His rhythms not only increase tensions but add a whole syncopative scheme to the tale, marking Collins's advances, his retreats as he walks toward his goal, and his final return to relative safety.

A clever little spoof, "An Indiana Campaign," tells the story of Major Tom Boldin, protector of the inhabitants of a small town during the Civil War. One warm summer day, while the Major is relaxing outside on a bench, a young boy rushes up to him to tell him a rebel is in town. Panic nearly breaks out in the streets as the news rapidly spreads. The entire village runs to the corn field where the "rebel" is supposed to be hiding. Crane builds suspense by taking time out to view "the gently swaying masses of corn, and behind them, the looming woods sinister with possible secrets." The Major and his aides cross through the field, climb the fence, peer into the underbrush, and listen. Suddenly they hear a noise. It is Old Milt Jacoby, the village drunk, not a rebel. Everyone in town expresses disappointment — the women more so than the men — as they "hurled this one superior sentence at the major: 'Well, yeh might have known.'" Crane's skill in describing the crescendo of collective fear, anger, and hatred and the dangers involved in such irrational outbreaks sets this tale apart from the others.

"A Grey Sleeve" is a sentimental tale about a Union officer who enters the home of a southern belle with his patrol. They want to search for the soldier wearing the grey sleeve whom they have seen through the window. Although suspenseful, as are many of Crane's tales, "A Grey Sleeve" is conventional, lacking the luster and meaningfulness of "The Little Regiment" and "A Mystery of Heroism." Even Crane saw the banality of the tale's romantic interlude, describing the Captain and the girl as "a pair of idiots." And though "there is something charming in their childish faith in each other," Crane had to admit to the fact that "A Grey Sleeve" was "not in any sense a good story . . . "[3]

"The Veteran" is the only short story in *The Little Regiment* that does not focus on the Civil War. It features Henry Fleming of *The Red Badge of Courage*, grown old. Promoted to orderly sergeant during the war, he now confesses to his grandson, who idolizes him and also harbors the same illusions Henry had when a callow youth, that he was afraid during combat and that he did run away from battle. This did not imply, he maintains, that he was not a good soldier. Sometimes the shock of awareness — the sudden realization that war is an abomination in which one can lose one's life — may have a strengthening effect; it may inspire one to fight harder and more courageously. This had been true in the young Fleming's case.

The second part of "The Veteran" takes place at night on Fleming's farm. The old man hears noises. His farmhand, a Swede, has thrown over a lantern by mistake and caused a fire in the barn. Fleming rushes out and saves the Swede. Then, despite warnings from his friends, he goes back into the barn to rescue two colts that are trapped in the burning building. "When the roof fell in, a great funnel of smoke swarmed toward the sky . . . the smoke was tinted rose-hue from the flames, and perhaps the unutterable midnights of the universe will have no power to daunt the color of this soul." With this Crane not only sums up his protagonist's heroic gesture but the poignancy of *feeling* in this old man who, at the outset of the tale, so movingly touched upon universal values and ideas in his conversations with his grandson.

The Little Regiment did receive some favorable reviews. Critics of the time singled out Crane's battle descriptions, his dramatic flair, his use of color in the splashes of brilliant and dismal hues, "like clippings out of the great book of war itself." These narrations about Fredericksburg and Chancellorsville however, are not his best. They are repetitions of what Crane said far more spectacularly in *The Red Badge of Courage*. Some critics considered *The Little Regiment*, "seriously handicapped by morbid psychology and by mannerism." Crane's impressionistic style was commendable and "his color-notation" fascinating, but frequently these things intruded on the story's action or character focus.

Cleverness and superb graphic descriptions are marred by "uniformly gruesome" themes and the sameness of the plots.

"An Episode of War"

"Episode of War" is a little masterpiece, not merely for its characterizations but for the melodic and visual beauty of its prose. War is depicted in all its dazzling violence as a glorious but viciously cruel experience. Like the paintings of artists such as Trumbull and Copley, Crane's tale is a powerful depiction of war.

A battery, a tumultuous and shining mass, was swirling toward the right. The wild thud of hoofs, the cries of the riders shouting blame and praise, menace and encouragement, and, last, the roar of the wheels, the slant of the glistening guns, brought the lieutenant to an intent pause. The battery swept in curves that stirred the heart; it made halts as dramatic as the crash of a wave on the rocks, and when it fled onward, this aggregation of wheels, levers, motors, had a beautiful unity, as if it were a missile. The sound of it was a war-chorus that reached into the depths of man's emotion.

As the story opens, a lieutenant is dividing the regiment's coffee rations and, in so doing, is "on the verge of a great triumph in mathematics." Suddenly a bullet strikes his arm. The men surrounding him are "astonished and awed by this catastrophe," *so unmathematical*, so unpredictable, so unexpected. As a result of this chance factor, everything in the lieutenant's life changes. He can't even grasp or sheath his sword. As he walks slowly and ponderously to the hospital, he wonders how he is going to tackle his new life. Outside the hospital, he sees a dying man who is calmly smoking his pipe. The sight of the man resigned to his fate encourages the lieutenant to face his own ordeal. Meeting the surgeon, who looks at him disdainfully and tells him to come along, he questions: "I guess I won't have it amputated?" Although the surgeon, accustomed to the fears of wounded men, reassures him, the lieutenant senses that he is entering "the portals of death." He imagines his family weeping as they look at his flat sleeve. "Oh, well, I don't suppose it matters so much as all that," he finally says.

The stoic reserve of the lieutenant and his courage in the face of adversity reflect Crane's belief that one learns to conform to new situations.

Wounds in the Rain

Wounds in the Rain is a collection of fictional tales based on Crane's reportages for the *World* and the *Journal* during what Crane called the "Cuban war." Although the stories are dramatic, ironic, and sometimes humorous, only three of the eleven are of high quality.

"The Price of the Harness" is one of the stronger stories. In it, Crane praises the soldier—the Regular—who shows the courage and fidelity demanded by his outfit. Ready to accept "the price of the harness," the regular is proud of being part of the military and adhering to its difficult regulations, but also willing to forego his freedom and even his life.

Nolan, Grierson, Watkins, and Martin are the four Regulars; they not only assume the responsibilities given them but thrive on this kind of regimentation. They obey their commanders without questioning, feel fraternity and respect for their fellow soldiers, and perform their tasks with skill and the stoicism that is implicit in their code of ethics. Antipodal to these Regulars are the poltroons and the naive, who not only lack judgment but also courage.

Although there are four protagonists in Crane's

tale, these characters actually compose one being, each having divested himself of his subjectivity, personal needs, and desires so as to fulfill the need of the collective. Few words are uttered among them as they work their long, hard hours, looking "indifferent, almost stolid, despite the heat and the labor." Crane takes the reader into the very heart of their routine existence. We listen to them talking about their food rations, sleeping habits, packing equipment, and armaments; we observe how they care for the wounded and react to the "doleful sobbing cry" of those who will die.

Nolan is shot during an encounter, but admits to no pain—only a numbness and a dampness in his back, surely because he is lying on wet ground. Grierson puts his hand under his friend's back. Removing his hand covered with blood, Grierson says nothing. Nolan closes his eyes "contentedly," just resting, never realizing he is dying. Nolan, Grierson, Watkins, and Martin are unsung heroes whom Crane deeply admires for their courage and their humility. Perhaps Crane longed to be one of them.

"The Lone Charge of William B. Perkins" depicts another military man, a war correspondent, William B. Perkins, who finds himself on a small dispatch-boat near the harbor at Guantánamo Bay. Certainly based on Crane's own war experiences, the story deals with marines encamped before a hill they are about to take and a correspondent, who longs to find out what he can about the men's feelings toward war and suffering.

"The Clan of No-Name" also deals with the war heroism of the Regulars but this time in a romantic context. Manolo, like Henry Fleming in *The Red Badge of Courage*, is new at the game of soldiering. Despite his inexperience, Manolo does assume the responsibilities—the "harness"—that the army's code requires. He joins the men of his regiment in a holding action, though he knows it to be futile. "There was a standard" which a soldier must follow and obey. The depiction of the savage nature of guerilla warfare in "The Clan of No-Name" is thrilling, as is the energetic delineation of that "mystic tie" that binds men in the throes of a struggle.

Crane's philosophical approach to war and his conception of conflict as not merely a human struggle but also a cosmic one are conveyed in the world of imponderables described in "The Price of the Harness" and in "The Lone Charge of William B. Perkins." Crane also intimates that the emotions endured during war—be they joyous or tragic—can never be conveyed to anyone who has not experienced them for himself.

That Crane was desperately ill when writing *Wounds in the Rain* is evident. His physical weakness and depression diminished whatever his imagination could have yielded. His powers were strained to their limits. As Crane wrote in the conclusion of "War Memories," "the episode was closed. And you can depend upon it that I have told you nothing at all, nothing at all, nothing at all."

Spitzbergen Tales

Revolving around a fictional Spitzbergen army, *Spitzbergen Tales* is comprised of four stories: "The Kicking Twelfth," "The Upturned Face," "The Shrapnel of their Friends," and "And If He Wills, We Must die." Each story dramatizes a different regimental episode during wartime; together they make up Crane's last portrait of war as a universal force. The ideal hero, Timothy Lean, who is present in all four tales, wants to fight; he dreams of skirmishes, valorous deeds, and excitement. But, like Henry Fleming at the outset of *The Red Badge of Courage*, he knows virtually nothing about the realities of war.

"The Upturned Face" is the finest of the four tales.

Utterly stark and simple, it focuses on one action, the burial of an officer. Lean and the adjutant must oversee the two privates who are digging the grave amidst a volley of bullet fire. The adjutant bursts "out in a sudden strange fury," telling them to hurry—they are "laboring for their lives." The hissing cacophonies of the exploding gun fire, together with the adjutant's own gutturals, add to the grim and frightening atmosphere of the episode. Lean orders the privates to take cover and picks up the shovel himself.

Soon there was nothing to be seen but the chalk-blue face. Lean filled his shovel. . . . "Good God," he cried to the adjutant. "Why didn't you turn him somehow when you put him in? This—" Then Lean began to stutter.

The adjutant understood. He was pale to the lips. "Go on, man," he cried beseechingly, almost in a shout. . . . Lean swung back the shovel; it went forward in a pendulum curve. When the earth landed it made a sound—plop.

Pain, fear, anguish are blended in this harrowing burial description, one of the most arresting of all Crane's images.

Both the adjutant and Lean were friends of the dead soldier, yet each views his task differently. The adjutant wants to leave the body unburied since the regiment is about to retreat—to remain in the line of fire is to take an unnecessary risk. Lean, guided by a sense of obligation, refuses to leave the body unburied. He does obey his superior officer who orders him to search the dead man's body, but his anguish is acute. Both Lean and the adjutant are horrified by the decomposing body and the finality of death. Anxiety mounts as dirt is shoveled first onto the feet and then the rest of the body. Each time the adjutant and Lean peer into the grave, they see themselves, unconsciously, in projection; they hesitate to cover one last part of the body—the face.

The build up in Crane's tale is monumental. The rhythmic power of the dirt being cast into the pit, the identification of the soldiers with the dead man, and their feelings of revulsion at the thought of the body's decomposition all add to a climax that transcends the individual act and takes on mythical stature. One wonders if Crane's grave illness made it possible for him to understand the *real* meaning of death and thus scale the heights of his narrative art.

11

The Monster and *The Whilomville Stories*

"The damned story has been haunting me. It's a subject for you," Joseph Conrad wrote Crane sometime after the American novelist had told him about "The Monster."[1]

"The Monster" is among Crane's finest and most sensitive works. His understanding of the functioning and motivations of human nature is impressive. The characters are adamantine in their clarity, and the episodes are harrowing and neatly woven together to form a cohesive whole. This long short story is particularly timely today when so much emphasis is being placed on the tormenting issues of keeping alive brain-dead people, mercy killings, transplants, cloaning, and robots. "The Monster" poses those eternal questions: What is the meaning of life? Is it the quality or the length of life that matters most?

"His New Mittens" (1898) is a subtle treatment of the feeling world of a seven-year-old boy. Crane writes his story with such finesse and warmth that one has the impression that it must be in part autobiographical.

Horace is walking home from school "brilliantly decorated by a pair of new red mittens." His friends call to him to join them in their "snow-balling." He has received, however, strict orders from his widowed mother and his maiden aunt to return home directly after school and to take care of his new red mittens. Watching his friends at play, Horace is torn between longing to join them and fear of his mother's admonition. Suddenly the children start to poke fun at him. "A-fray-ed of his mittens! A-fray-ed of his mit-tens!" they scream gleefully with no uncertain amount of resentment against the outsider.

To be the butt of ridicule makes Horace feel even worse; he "cast[s] a tortured glance" toward the children. Then he drops "his eyes to the snow at his feet," making believe he is examining the bark of the tree. His loneliness tears him apart. He is not yet strong enough to stand the derisive, taunting, and sarcastic ways of his peers. He gruffly answers their sharp cries, denying the fact that he is not playing with them for fear of wetting his mittens. "Tain't them I care bout," he retorts. "I've got to go home. That's all." The children start their taunts again. As he stands there, "a mere baby, outflanked him and then struck him in the cheek with a heavy snow-ball." The baby retreats and is complimented by the other children for his courage.

Moments later, something catches the attention of the children a they are off on another adventure. Horace needs time to think, to "adjust his self-respect." He feels different. He has learned something. Still loitering about, watching the boys in their new game, he doesn't rush home. But a sense of guilt and of "impending punishment for disobedience" hangs over him. Suddenly his friends run by and again cry out their refrain, "A-fray-ed of his mit-tens!" This time the pain Horace feels is too much to bear. He bends down, scoops up some snow, molds it into a ball, and throws it at his enemy. It reaches its target. The boys take sides. The fight is on.

Soon Horace hears "a certain familiar tune of two notes, with the last note shrill and prolonged." It is his mother calling to him from the sidewalk. He turns around. She orders him home, her "inexorable profile" plunging into him like a dagger thrust. At home, his mother asks him for his mittens. When he fails to produce them, she finds them in his pocket and her face grows sad. Then Horace bursts into tears. His punishment: to remain on his chair until his mother tells him he can get up. When she brings him supper, Horace is overcome with feelings of anger and resentment. Wanting to take revenge on his mother for such mistreatment he refuses to eat his supper, knowing that to do so will worry his mother. This is only the beginning of his plan of attack.

Horace decides to run away to "a remote corner of the world." His mother will never know what happened to him; nor will his aunt remain unscathed. Horace gets up, puts on his coat and cap, and decides to go to California. Although it is snowing very hard, he walks to the street and makes his way to Stickney's butcher shop where he tells the amazed butcher that he has run away from home. Tears pour down his face. This kindly paternal man takes the lad home. No sooner does Horace see his mother "lying limp, pale as death, her eyes gleaming with pain," then he runs to her crying "Mama!" Unable to speak, she enfolds him in her arms.

The maiden aunt's last statement pronounced in a "half military, half feminine" voice sums up the meaning of the tale. Turning away from the butcher lest he see her tears, she says, "Won't you have a glass of our root-beer, Mr. Stickney. We make it ourselves". The implication is that this matriarchal fold, as represented by mother and aunt, is responsible for the child's suffering. The patriarchal power needed so desperately in the family is represented by the warm and understanding butcher.

Horace, being a boy himself, "did not understand boys at all" — a statement Crane could make because his knowledge of adolescents was so keen. He felt deeply that children need snow-ball fights or "war games" to purge themselves of their anger and frustrations. Indeed, had Crane ever outgrown his youthful world of boxing, fighting, and whooping it up? Had he ever reached maturity with its obligations and commitments? He lived intensely and understood malevolence and benevolence in human nature. Yet, this eternal boy slipped back into childhood with ease, regressing into a period in his life when the world — though not always a happy one — seemed relatively pleasant and simple.

Crane is one of those masters who are able to depict the complex world of boyhood with its loves and hates, aggressions, fantasies, and whimsies. Masters such as Mark Twain, William Dean Howells, Thomas Bailey Aldrich, and, later, Booth Tarkington have invited their readers to share in the child's world of mystery, fantasy and magic.

The Whilomville Stories, published posthumously in 1900, consists of thirteen tales Crane wrote during the last year of his life. The work deals exclusively with boyhood, that time which an adult looks back upon as filled with great expectations. The stories are drawn from events and escapades occurring in Port Jervis, where Crane had lived from the age of seven to twelve. The author wanted the stories to appear as a series covering a thirteen-month period from 1899–1900.[2] And so their time scheme is chronological, beginning in the summer months and including two Christmas holidays.

Why Crane wrote these stories at the end of his life is an interesting question. Living at Brede Place and plagued with imminent bankruptcy, Crane may have found that writing the *Whilomville Stories* took him back to a relatively carefree, if not happy, period. Other factors may also have made him turn to the past. Cora had taken in Crane's friend, Harold Frederic's second household, Kate Lyon and her three children, who were aged seven, five, and four. The lively presence of the children may have encouraged Crane to return to his beginnings—to Whilomville. The results, from a literary point of view were not, however, the best. His sickness and enormous commitments and responsibilities may have drained his creative elan. Still, he continued writing these tales to the end of his life.

The Whilomville Stories, with their close-ups of small-town America, focus on the individual and the collective. Whilomville could have been Hawthorne's Salem, or Henry James's Woollett, with all of those towns' righteousness, rigid codes, and so-called ethics. The stories open up the child's mysterious world to the readers: the boy countering the domination of his parents, the gender and generation gaps, and the hatreds and loves these conflicts elicit. In all of the stories—which include "The Angel Child," "Lynx-Hunting," "The Lover and the Tell-Tale," "The Carriage-Lamps," "The Knife," "The Stove," and "The Fight"—we are made privy to hurt, innocence, pride, hypocrisy, and restrictions. The world of play, of innocence, whimsy, glee, and rambunctiousness, is presented in a complex of coruscating feelings. In Crane's world, the child is still that fabulous being, struggling to liberate himself from his fold, yet remaining within its confines, since he is not yet strong enough to take that lunge into life. Both bold and timid, the young boy is a composite of opposites. He must be taken seriously, studied, and analyzed for within him lurks the traits of the man he will become: love and hate, passivity and aggression, brutality and kindliness, savagery and civility. Which parts of his personality will emerge in later life? This is the question Crane attempts to answer, and he succeeds in conveying its poignancy to his readers in these haunting and beguiling tales.

Although not Crane's best stylistically speaking

and flawed, perhaps, by their sentimentality and frailty of content, *The Whilomville Stories* are, nevertheless, deeply perceptive. As the reviewer for the *Academy* suggested, Crane's treatment of children was meaningful to many a reader, for "in the minute touches by which his ultra-sensitized mind reflected the humours, the gaieties, the bizarreries of the struggle against an armed landscape that is modern war, you find the marks of the wonderful beyondness that was his convincing effect."[3]

Conclusion

What remains to be said of Crane's writings today? What factors does this nineteenth-century American writer trigger in the contemporary reader's mind, imagination, and sensibilities that make his writings so vibrantly fascinating?

Crane's style and his themes, his powerful, incisive, brilliantly colorful, imagistic, and rhythmic prose embeds itself deeply in the souls of those reading his books today. Unforgettable are the epithets that serve to depict his nameless and eternal beings in *The Red Badge of Courage*. No longer are we faced with the hero: the young man able to dominate his fate, forge ahead, win battle upon battle and then take pride in his achievements—become emblazoned in an ideal. Instead, Crane dared depict the *anti-hero*, the one who failed to live up to the image society creates and the one that he would like to have of himself. His anti-hero does evolve, he does mature—slowly, not drastically, painfully, but not completely, as he learns to accept his weaknesses. And, by the same token, the new insights he develops help him deal with his own problems.

Antithetical metaphorical images and rhythms in most all of Crane's novels, short stories and poems, serve to dramatize situations, to create tensions, to exacerbate sensibilities. In "The Open Boat," water and land, life and death, serenity and violence are juxtaposed, as Crane slowly but relentlessly discloses the meaning of *dread*, with his pictorial depictions of sweeping seas that threaten to send the little boat with its survivors down to the ocean floor. In "The Blue Hotel," heat and snow, love and hate, are accompanied by a variety of rhythmic clauses, black-and-white shadings, which heighten the drama of the moment and serve to depict the inner man as he expels his rage in his fight for retribution.

The inability of parents to understand their children and to work at cross-purposes is dramatized in *George's Mother*. Rarely has a mother figure been depicted in such an acidulous and graphic manner. She fits the description of the hateful, insidious, vicious woman ready and able to crush the nascent child and the weakly structured youth.

Compassion for the poor, the unfortunate, the pariahs of this earth — the Bowery bums, the prostitutes, the addicts, alcoholics, the criminal, and the supercilious clergymen, the do-gooders — are all relentlessly subsumed in *Maggie: A Girl of the Streets* and in "An Experiment in Misery," and many other of Crane's short stories and reportages.

A love for nature, animals, sports, and children has never been better sensed than in Crane's "Sullivan County Sketches," *Plain Tales*, and *The Whilomville Stories*. Though an outstanding spinner of yarns, Crane's themes could be considered slight, dealing with fishing, camping, hunting, and games. But the tensions he generates in "The Pace of Youth," "Death and the Child," "The Monster," and the compassion he thereby elicits create parallel feelings in the reader's psyche.

Crane's meditations on war, on life and death in such poems as "War is Kind," set up trenchant and brutal vibrations in the reader. His accumulation of grim clusters of unorthodox structural units, alliterations, and onomatopoeia — unorthodox for the period, but timely today — create dissonant or mellifluous tonal variations in increasing varieties of modulations.

Any consideration of style and theme must include Crane's "anti-God" poems. Beginning with hymnlike majesty, they build with frenzied amplitudes, reaching apocalyptic dimension, as Crane, the poet, the seer, castigates the Evil God who wreaks havoc upon his creation—maiming, killing, encouraging a world rife with contention to pursue its bloodbaths.

Crane banished the banner of illusions. No more sugar-coated pills are to be handed out. Realist, perhaps, but Symbolist, and Expressionist as well, he appeals today because he answers a need in contemporary humanity. Speaking out forcefully and powerfully— and in so doing, thrashing out the cruelties pervading contemporary societies throughout the world—this was Crane's way of righting a wrong, of branding those who seek to destroy, to dominate, to convert people to their sacrosanct but hideously distorted views. They debase the name of God. They are the ones Crane sought to denounce and to unmask. Speaking courageously against the power hungry—be it for political or religious reasons—so he articulates, just as powerfully and longingly, on love and relatedness.

Crane, the creator of literary monuments to eternity, reaches out to young and old today as he had in his own time: truthfully, overtly, passionately. No one but Crane could be better called the purveyor of Samuel Johnson's dictum: "In order that all men may be taught to speak truth, it is necessary that all likewise should learn to hear it."

Notes

INTRODUCTION

1. "H. G. Wells on Stephen Crane," *Stephen Crane's Career*. Edited by Thomas A. Gullason, p. 133.
2. "Joseph Conrad on Stephen Crane," *Stephen Crane's Career*, p. 136.

1. THE STORY OF HIS LIFE

1. *Stephen Crane: Letters*. Edited by R. W. Stallman and Lilian Gilkes, p. 119, (To Viola Allen, Mar. 15, 1896).
2. R. W. Stallman, *Stephen Crane: A Biography*, p. 28.
3. Ibid., pp. 24–46.
4. Howells, William Dean, "The Editor's Study," *Harper's Monthly* (Apr. 1877). (Quoted in *Norton Anthology of American Literature*, Ronald Gottesman, et al. eds., p. 971.
5. *Letters*, p. 100, (To Helen Trent, Sept. 20, 1981).
6. *The Works of Stephen Crane*, Vol. 7, *Tales, Sketches and Reports*. Intro. by Edwin H. Cady. (All subsequent quotes are taken from this section.)
7. *Letters*, pp. 31–32, (To Mrs. Lily Brandon Munroe, Mar. 1894).
8. Ibid.
9. "An Experiment in Misery," New York *Press* (Apr. 22, 1894). "Men in the Storm," *Arena* (Oct. 1894).
10. *Letters*, p. 115 (To Nellie Crouse, Feb. 11, 1896).
11. Ibid., p. 99, (To Nellie Crouse, Jan. 12, 1896).
12. Ibid., p. 120, (To Nellie Crouse, Mar. 1 and 18, 1896).
13. Stallman, p. 189. Edwin H. Cady, *Stephen Crane*, pp. 49–52.
14. Stallman, p. 222.
15. Ibid., pp. 220–32.

16. Ibid., p. 296.
17. "William Dean Howells on Stephen Crane," *Stephen Crane's Career*. Edited by Thomas A. Gullason, p. 93.
18. Stallman, p. 239.
19. *Letters*, p. 132, (To Cora Taylor, November 1896).
20. Stallman, p. 254.
21. Ibid., p. 269.
22. Ibid., p. 276.
23. Ibid., p. 275.
24. Ibid., p. 298.
25. Ibid., p. 321.
26. *Letters*, p. 150, (To Joseph Conrad, Nov. 11, 1897).
27. Stallman, pp. 302, 323.
28. Ibid., p. 316.
29. Ibid., p. 347.
30. Ibid., p. 352.
31. Ibid., p. 359.
32. Ibid., p. 362.
33. Ibid., pp. 368–71.

2. MAGGIE: A GIRL OF THE STREETS

1. *Stephen Crane: Letters*, p. 14, (To Hamlin Garland, Mar. [?] 1893).
2. R. W. Stallman, *Stephen Crane: A Biography*, p. 66.
3. *Stephen Crane: An Omnibus*. Edited by R. W. Stallman, p. 103.
4. *Stephen Crane: A Biography*, p. 69.
5. *Letters*, p. 133, (To Miss Catherine Harris, Nov. 12[?], 1896).
6. Ibid., ". . . perhaps you have been informed that I am not very friendly to Christianity as seen around town."
7. John Berryman, *Stephen Crane*, p. 21.
8. Stallman, p. 539.

3. THE RED BADGE OF COURAGE

1. *Stephen Crane: Letters*, p. 78.
2. Ibid., p. 158.
3. Ibid., p. 50.

4. Ibid., p. 8.
5. Russell Lynes, *The Art Makers of Nineteenth-Century America*, p. 343.
6. Joseph Conrad, "His War Book," *Stephen Crane*. Edited by Maurice Bassan, p. 124.

4. GEORGE'S MOTHER

1. *The Works of Stephen Crane*. vol. I. "An Ambitious French Novel and a Modest American Story," *Arena*, June 1893.
2. *Stephen Crane: Letters*, p. 41, (To Hamlin Garland, Nov. 15, 1894).
3. Robert L. Hough, "Crane and Goethe: A Forgotten Relationship," *Stephen Crane's Career*. Edited by Thomas A. Gullason, p. 191.
4. *The Works of Stephen Crane*. Vol. 1. Introduction by James B. Colvert, p. 108.
5. Donald B. Gibson, *The Fiction of Stephen Crane*, p. 50. *The Work of Stephen Crane* vol. I, p. 104; Stallman, *Stephen Crane: A Biography*, pp. 213–16.

5. THE THIRD VIOLET

1. *Stephen Crane: Letters*, p. 106, (To Ripley Hitchcock, Jan. 27, 1896).
2. "Hamlin Garland on Stephen Crane," *Stephen Crane's Career*. Edited by Thomas A. Gullason, p. 99.
3. Lewis Mumford, *The Brown Decades*.
4. *Letters*, pp. 78–79.
5. Stallman, pp. 295–98. H. G. Wells, "Stephen Crane from an English Standpoint," in *Stephen Crane: Letters*, p. 315. *The Works of Stephen Crane*, Vol. 3, *The Third Violet* and *Active Service*. Introduction by J. C. Levenson.

6. ACTIVE SERVICE

1. R. W. Stallman, *Stephen Crane: A Biography*, p. 472.

2.   Ibid., p. 600.

7. THE O'RUDDY

1.   R. W. Stallman, *Stephen Crane: A Biography*, p. 558.

8. THE BLACK RIDERS AND WAR IS KIND

1.   Ralph Waldo Emerson, "Self-Reliance," *The Norton Anthology of American Literature*, p. 311.
2.   *Stephen Crane: Letters*, p. 79, (To an Editor of *Leslie's Weekly*, Nov. 1895).
3.   R. W. Stallman, *Stephen Crane: A Biography*, p. 89.
4.   Ibid., pp. 125, 157.
5.   Edward Garnett, "Stephen Crane: An Appreciation," *Stephen Crane's Career*. Edited by Thomas A. Gullason, p. 143.
6.   Daniel Hoffman, *The Poetry of Stephen Crane*, pp. 25–45.

9. TALES OF ADVENTURE

1.   Edgar Allan Poe's review of Nathaniel Hawthorne's *Tales* (1842).
2.   *Stephen Crane: Letters*, p. 69, (To Willis Brooks Hawkins, Nov. 5, 1895).
3.   R. W. Stallman, *Stephen Crane: An Omnibus of Crane*, pp. 448–76.
4.   Herman Melville, *Moby-Dick*, chap. 1.
5.   *Stephen Crane: Letters*, p. 312. H. G. Wells, "Stephen Crane from an English Standpoint." (First published in the *North American Review*, Aug. 1900.)

10. TALES OF WAR

1.   *Stephen Crane: Letters*, p. 72 (To Willis Brooks Hawkins, Nov. 12, 1895).

2.   Stallman, *Stephen Crane: A Biography*, pp. 546, 548.
3.   *Letters*, p. 97, (To Nellie Crouse, Jan. 6, 1896).

11. THE MONSTER AND THE WHILOMVILLE
STORIES

1.   *Letters*, p. 169, (Joseph Conrad to Stephen Crane, Jan. 16, 1898).
2.   *The Works of Stephen Crane*, Vol. 7, *Tales of Whilomville*.
3.   R. W. Stallman, *Stephen Crane*, p. 483.

Bibliography

PRIMARY SOURCES

The Works of Stephen Crane. Edited by Fredson Bowers. Charlottesville: University Press of Virginia. Vol. 1, *Bowery Tales*, Intro. by James B. Colvert, 1969. Vol. 2, *The Red Badge of Courage*, Intro. by J. C. Levenson, 1975. Vol. 3, *The Third Violet*, Intro. by J. C. Levenson, 1976. Vol. 4. *The O'Ruddy*, Intro. by J. C. Levenson, 1971. Vol. 5, *Tales of Adventure*, Intro. by J. C. Levenson, 1970. Vol. 6, *Tales of War*, Intro. by James B. Colvert, 1970. Vol. 7, *Tales of Whilomville*, Intro. by J. C. Levenson, 1969. Vol. 8, *Tales, Sketches, and Reports*, Intro. by Edwin H. Cady, 1973. Vol. 10, *Poems and Literary Remains*, Intro. by James B. Colvert, 1975.

SECONDARY SOURCES

Ahnebrink, Lars. *The Beginnings of Naturalism in American Fiction*. Cambridge, Mass.: Harvard University Press, 1950.

Bassan, Maurice, ed. *Stephen Crane: A Collection of Critical Essays*. Englewood Cliffs, New Jersey: Prentice-Hall, 1967.

Beer, Thomas. *Stephen Crane, A Study in American Letters*. New York: Alfred A. Knopf, Inc., 1923.

Bergon, Frank. *Stephen Crane's Artistry*. New York: Columbia University Press, 1975.

Berryman, John. *Stephen Crane*. New York: William Sloane Associates, 1950.

Brooks, Van Wyck. *The Confident Years: 1885–1915*. New York: Dutton, 1952.

Cady, Edwin H. *Stephen Crane*. New York: Gosset and Dunlap, 1962.

————., and Lester G. Wells, eds. *Stephen Crane's Love Letters to Nellie Crouse*, Syracuse, New York: Syracuse University Press, 1954.

Geismar, Maxwell. *Rebels and Ancestors: The American Novel 1890-1915*. Boston: Houghton-Mifflin, 1953.

Gibson, Donald B. *The Fiction of Stephen Crane*. Carbondale: Southern Illinois University Press, 1968.

Gilkes, Lilian. *Cora Crane*. Bloomington: Indiana University Press, 1960.

Gullason, Thomas A., ed. *Stephen Crane's Career*. New York: New York University Press, 1972.

Hoffman, Daniel. *The Poetry of Stephen Crane*. New York: Columbia University Press, 1963.

Holtin, Milne. *Cylinder of Vision*. Baton Rouge: Louisiana State University Press, 1972.

La France, Marston. *A Reading of Stephen Crane*. Oxford: Clarendon Press, 1971.

Linson, Corwin Knapp. *My Stephen Crane*, ed. Edwin H. Cady. Syracuse: Syracuse University Press, 1957.

Lively, Robert A. *Fiction Fights the Civil War*. Chapel Hill: University of North Carolina Press, 1957.

Solomon, Eric. *Stephen Crane: From Parody to Realism*. Cambridge, Mass.: Harvard University Press, 1966.

Stallman, R. W. *Stephen Crane: A Biography*. New York: George Braziller, 1968.

————., ed. *Stephen Crane: An Omnibus*. New York: Alfred A. Knopf, 1952.

————., and Lilian Gilkes, eds. *Stephen Crane: Letters*. New York: New York University Press, 1960.

Taylor, Gordon O. *The Passages of Thought: Psychological Representation in the American Novel, 1870-1900*. New York: Oxford University Press, 1969.

Van Doren, Carl. Introduction to *The Works of Stephen Crane*, Vol. 4. New York: Knopf, 1925-27.

Walcutt, Charles C. *American Literary Naturalism: A Divided Stream*. Minneapolis: University Press, 1956.

Ziff, Larzer. *The American 1890's: Life and Times of a Lost Generation*. New York: Viking, 1966.

Index